The Ultimate Cuisinart Air Fryer Oven Cookbook for Beginners

250 Delicious Recipes for Your Cuisinart Air Fryer Toaster Oven

Jessie Owen

CONTENTS

Meat Recipes... 72

Fish & Seafood 81

Meatless Recipes 88

INTRODUCTION

If you want to whip up delicious, nutritious, tasty meals with a single touch of a button, you need an oven that can toast and air fry. The Cuisinart Air Fryer Toaster Oven does just that - it serves not only as an air frier but also as a fast and efficient electric oven and a toaster. Spend less time in your kitchen and enjoy your loved ones while the marvelous Cuisinart cooks some crispy chicken with french fries. It can also broil, bake, or warm, and all this in a single kitchen appliance. A little too much information for you? Don't worry, as this cookbook will guide you through the process of taking advantage of your cooking appliance.

Cuisinart Air Fryer Toaster Oven is a unique kitchen machine, and a full-size toasting oven with an air fryer built-in. So it not only broils, bakes and toasts, but it will also let you air fry right inside the oven. With the air frying function, you can cook delicious fried meals, such as wings, fritters, fries, or shrimp, more healthily, thanks to its powerful hot-air technology. Say bye to messy cleanups and say hi to crunchy and crispy experiences without the extra calories, with the new Cuisinart Air Fryer Toaster Oven.

Why this cookbook?

This cookbook encompasses a wide variety of recipes that are easy to follow and, most importantly, very easy to cook inside your Air Fryer oven. This book is meant to be a guide to you as you explore the novelty of the Cuisinart Air Fryer Oven. My goal is that you will be able to make some sumptuous meals without the pain of spending many hours in the kitchen. You will find that the ingredients used here are easy to find, and the cooking process is straightforward. Most of the recipes cook in less than one hour, which is the main reason this kitchen appliance was invented - to cook faster than a traditional oven.

FUNCTIONS AND BENEFITS

Power On Light - This Indicator lights up when in use

ON/Oven Timer Dial - Use to set the desired time for all functions except Toast function. Setting the oven timer powers the unit on and begins the cooking cycle. When the timer runs out, the unit will power off.

Oven Temperature Dial - set the desired temperature.

Function Dial - select cooking settings – Warm, Bake, Broil, AirFry, etc.

ON/Toast Timer Dial - choose desired toasting shade from lighter to darker.

Pull Out Crumb Tray - it comes positioned inside the oven. It comes out from the bottom front of the oven for convenient cleaning.

Air Fryer Basket - use the basket on AirFry setting for the optimal cooking outcome. Always use nested in the baking pan.

Oven Rack - use in two positions: bottom or top.

Drip Tray/Baking Bpan - this equipment is included in the package. Use it when or roasting or baking, and with the frying basket when AirFrying.

BREAKFAST

Banana & Peanut Butter Cake

Prep + Cook Time: 30 minutes | Serves: 4

Ingredients

¼ cup vegetable oil
1 cup flour
¼ tsp baking soda
1 tsp baking powder
⅓ cup sugar
2 mashed bananas

1 egg, beaten
1 tsp vanilla extract
¾ cup chopped walnuts
¼ tsp salt
2 tbsp peanut butter
2 tbsp sour cream

Directions

Preheat Cuisinart on Bake function to 350 F. Spray a 9-inch baking pan with cooking spray or grease with butter. Combine the flour, salt, baking powder, and baking soda in a bowl.

In another bowl, combine bananas, oil, egg, peanut butter, vanilla, sugar, and sour cream. Gently combine both mixtures. Stir in the chopped walnuts. Pour the batter into the pan. Cook for 20 minutes. Let cool completely and serve sliced.

Morning Blueberry Muffins

Prep + Cook Time: 35 minutes | Serves: 6

Ingredients

¼ cup coconut oil, melted
1 cup flour
½ cup dark brown sugar
1 tsp baking powder
1 tsp ground cinnamon
¼ tbsp vanilla extract

¼ tsp salt
1 cup blueberries
⅓ cup shredded, sweetened coconut
2 large eggs
Juice and zest of ½ orange

Directions

Preheat Cuisinart on Bake function to 360 F. In a mixing bowl, thoroughly combine the flour, brown sugar, baking powder, cinnamon, vanilla, and salt. Fold in the blueberries and coconut and toss to combine well.

In a different bowl, whisk eggs, coconut oil, orange juice, and orange zest. Add the wet mixture to the dry ingredients and mix again. Spoon the batter into greased muffin cups. Bake for 25 minutes; poke a toothpick in the center to make sure they're done. Cool before serving.

Lemon Cupcakes with Cream Cheese Frosting

Prep + Cook Time: 35 minutes | Serves: 6

Ingredients

Lemon Frosting:

3 tbsp icing sugar

1 lemon, zested

1 tbsp lemon juice

3 crystallized ginger slices, chopped

5 oz cream cheese, softened

Cupcake:

½ cup butter, softened

2 lemons, juiced

1 tbsp lemon zest

1 ½ cups flour + extra for basing

¼ tsp salt

1 cup sugar

1 tsp baking powder

1 tsp vanilla extract

2 eggs

½ cup milk

Directions

Beat the butter and sugar with an electric mixer until creamed. Fold in the eggs, one at a time, mixing constantly at low speed. Sift the flour, baking powder, and salt and mix well.

Stir the dry ingredients into the wet ingredients and slowly add the lemon juice, milk, lemon zest, and vanilla; beat on low speed until creamy and uniform.

Preheat Cuisinart on Bake function to 360 F. Line a muffin pan with 12 liners and spoon the batter into the cases ¾ way up. Place them in the Air Fryer tray and bake for 20-22 minutes. Once ready, remove, and let cool completely.

In a bowl, whisk cream cheese and icing sugar. Add in the lemon zest and lemon juice and stir to combine. Design the cupcakes with the frosting, top with the crystallized ginger and serve.

Nutmeg Potato Gratin

Prep + Cook Time: 35 minutes | Serves: 5

Ingredients

5 large potatoes

½ cup sour cream

½ cup grated cheddar cheese

½ cup milk

½ tsp nutmeg

Salt and black pepper to taste

Directions

Preheat Cuisinart on Bake function to 375 F. Peel and slice the potatoes. In a bowl, combine the sour cream, milk, pepper, salt, and nutmeg. Add in the potato slices and stir to coat well. Transfer the mixture to an ovenproof casserole. Cook for 15 minutes, then sprinkle the cheese on top and cook for 10 more minutes. Allow sitting for 10 minutes before serving.

Crunchy Asparagus with Cheese

Prep + Cook Time: 20 minutes | Serves: 4

Ingredients

1 lb asparagus spears
¼ cup flour
1 cup breadcrumbs

½ cup Parmesan cheese, grated
2 eggs, beaten
Salt and black pepper to taste

Directions

Preheat Cuisinart on Air Fry function to 370 F. Combine the breadcrumbs and Parmesan cheese in a bowl. Season with salt and pepper. Line a baking sheet with parchment paper. Dip the asparagus spears into the flour first, then into the eggs, and finally coat with the crumbs.

Arrange them on the AirFryer Basket, fit in the baking sheet, and cook for about 8 to 10 minutes. Serve with melted butter, hollandaise sauce, or freshly squeezed lemon.

Raspberry Maple Pancakes

Prep + Cook Time: 25 minutes | Serves: 4

Ingredients

2 cups all-purpose flour
1 cup milk
3 eggs, beaten
1 tsp baking powder
1 cup brown sugar

1 ½ tsp vanilla extract
½ cup frozen raspberries, thawed
2 tbsp maple syrup
A pinch of salt

Directions

Preheat Cuisinart on Bake function to 400 F. In a bowl, mix the flour, baking powder, salt, milk, eggs, vanilla extract, and brown sugar until smooth. Stir in the raspberries. Do it gently to avoid coloring the batter. Drop the batter onto a greased cooking pan. Make sure to leave some space between the pancakes. Cook for 10-15 minutes. Drizzle with maple syrup and serve.

Apricot Scones with Almonds

Prep + Cook Time: 35 minutes | Serves: 4

Ingredients

¼ cup cold butter, cut into cubes
2 cups flour
⅓ cup sugar
2 tsp baking powder
½ cup sliced almonds

¾ cup chopped dried apricots
½ cup milk
1 egg
1 tsp vanilla extract

Directions

Preheat Cuisinart on Bake function to 360 F. Line a large baking sheet with parchment paper. Mix together flour, sugar, baking powder, almonds, and apricots. Rub the butter into the dry ingredients with hands to form a sandy, crumbly texture. Whisk together egg, milk, and vanilla.

Pour into the dry ingredients and stir to combine. Sprinkle a working board with flour, lay the dough onto the board, and give it a few kneads. Shape into a rectangle and cut into 8 squares. Arrange the squares on the baking sheet and cook for 20-25 minutes.

Vanilla Brownies with White Chocolate & Walnuts

Prep + Cook Time: 30 minutes | Serves: 4

Ingredients

6 oz butter
6 oz dark chocolate, chopped
¾ cup white sugar
3 eggs, beaten
2 tsp vanilla extract

¾ cup flour
¼ cup cocoa powder
1 cup chopped walnuts
1 cup white chocolate chips

Directions

Line a baking pan with parchment paper. In a saucepan, melt chocolate and butter over low heat. Do not stop stirring until you obtain a smooth mixture. Let cool slightly and whisk in eggs and vanilla. Sift flour and cocoa into a bowl. Add the egg mixture and sugar and stir to mix well.

Sprinkle the walnuts over and add the white chocolate into the batter. Pour the batter into the baking pan and cook for 20 minutes in the Cuisinart oven at 350 F on Bake function. Serve chilled.

Olive & Tomato Tart with Feta Cheese

Prep + Cook Time: 25 minutes | Serves: 2

Ingredients

2 tbsp olive oil
4 eggs
½ cup tomatoes, chopped
1 cup feta cheese, crumbled
1 tbsp fresh basil, chopped

1 tbsp fresh oregano, chopped
¼ cup Kalamata olives, chopped
¼ cup onion, chopped
½ cup milk
Salt and black pepper to taste

Directions

Preheat Cuisinart on Bake function to 360 F. Brush a pie pan with olive oil. Beat the eggs along with the milk, salt, and pepper. Stir in all of the remaining ingredients. Pour the egg mixture into the pan. Cook for 20 minutes. Serve warm.

Breaded Cauliflowers in Alfredo Sauce

Prep + Cook Time: 25 minutes | Serves: 4

Ingredients

1 tbsp butter, melted
4 cups cauliflower florets
¼ cup alfredo sauce

1 cup breadcrumbs
1 tsp sea salt

Directions

Whisk the alfredo sauce along with the butter. In a shallow bowl, combine the breadcrumbs with the sea salt. Dip each cauliflower floret into the alfredo mixture first, and then coat with the crumbs. Drop the prepared florets into the fryer basket. Fit in the baking tray.

Set the temperature of your Cuisinart to 380 F and cook for 15 minutes on Air Fry function. Shake the florets twice during cooking. Serve.

Cheesy Eggs with Fried Potatoes

Prep + Cook Time: 30 minutes | Serves: 4

Ingredients

1 tbsp olive oil
2 lb potatoes, thinly sliced
2 eggs, beaten
2 oz cheddar cheese, grated

1 tbsp all-purpose flour
½ cup coconut cream
Salt and black pepper to taste

Directions

Season the potatoes with salt and pepper and place them in the fryer basket; drizzle with olive oil. Fit in the baking tray and cook in your Cuisinart for 12 minutes at 350 F on Air Fry function.

Mix the eggs, coconut cream, and flour in a bowl until well blended. Remove the potatoes from the fryer oven, line them in a baking pan and top with the cream mixture. Sprinkle with cheddar cheese. Cook for 12 more minutes. Serve warm.

Orange French Toast

Prep + Cook Time: 25 minutes | Serves: 2

Ingredients

2 fresh eggs
¼ cup milk
1 tbsp orange juice
1 tsp orange zest

1 tsp vanilla extract
¼ tsp ground cinnamon
4 bread slices
2 tbsp cranberry jelly

Directions

Preheat Cuisinart on Air Fry function to 360 F. Line a baking sheet with parchment paper and spritz with cooking spray. In a mixing bowl, beat the eggs, milk, orange juice, orange zest, vanilla, and cinnamon. Dip the bread slices into the egg mixture, coating well on both sides. Let the excess liquid drip off, then put them on the baking sheet. Bake for 14-16 minutes, turning once until golden brown and crispy. Serve hot topped with cranberry jelly.

Creamy Bacon & Egg Tortillas

Prep + Cook Time: 15 minutes | Serves: 3

Ingredients

3 tortillas
2 previously scrambled eggs
3 slices bacon, cut into strips

3 tbsp salsa
3 tbsp cream cheese, divided
1 cup grated Monterey Jack cheese

Directions

Preheat Cuisinart on Air Fry to 390 F. Spread cream cheese onto the tortillas. Divide the eggs and bacon between the tortillas. Top with salsa. Sprinkle with Monterey Jack cheese. Roll up the tortillas. Place in a greased baking pan and cook for 10 minutes. Serve.

Mom's Apple Fritters

Prep + Cook Time: 20 minutes | Serves: 4

Ingredients

1 lb apples, peeled and grated
¼ cup cornflour
1 cup flour
⅓ cup sugar
2 tsp baking powder

1 tsp pumpkin pie spice
⅛ tsp salt
½ cup apple juice
1 fresh egg, beaten
2 tbsp honey

Directions

Preheat Cuisinart oven on Air Fry function to 350 F. Line a baking sheet with parchment paper and spritz with cooking spray. Add the cornflour, flour, sugar, baking powder, pumpkin pie spice, and salt to a bowl and mix well. Drain the excess liquid out of the apples and add them to the bowl; stir to combine.

In a different bowl, blend the apple juice and egg. Add the wet mixture to the dry ingredients and mix again to combine well. Shape the mixture into tablespoon-sized cakes, then place them on the baking sheet. Spritz with cooking spray and air fry for 5 minutes. Flip the fritters and cook for another 5 minutes, or until golden.Drizzle with honey and serve. Enjoy!

Savory Cheddar & Cauliflower Tater Tots

Prep + Cook Time: 20 minutes | Serves: 4

Ingredients

2 lb cauliflower florets, steamed
5 oz cheddar cheese, shredded
1 onion, diced
1 cup breadcrumbs
1 egg, beaten

1 tsp fresh parsley, chopped
1 tsp fresh oregano, chopped
1 tsp fresh chives, chopped
1 tsp garlic powder
Salt and black pepper to taste

Directions

Mash the cauliflower and place it in a large bowl. Add in the onion, parsley, oregano, chives, garlic powder, salt, pepper, and cheddar cheese. Mix with your hands until thoroughly combined and form 12 balls out of the mixture. Line a baking sheet with parchment paper.

Dip half of the tater tots into the egg and then coat with breadcrumbs. Arrange them on the AirFryer Basket and spray with cooking spray. Fit in the baking sheet and cook in the Cuisinart oven at 390 minutes for 10-12 minutes on Air Fry function. Serve.

Corn & Chorizo Frittata

Prep + Cook Time: 35 minutes | Serves: 4

Ingredients

1 tbsp olive oil
6 eggs
2 large potatoes, boiled and cubed
½ cup frozen corn

½ cup feta cheese, crumbled
1 tbsp fresh parsley, chopped
½ chorizo, sliced
Salt and black pepper to taste

Directions

Preheat Cuisinart on Air Fry function to 375 F. Heat the olive oil in a skillet over medium heat and cook the chorizo for 3 minutes. Beat the eggs with salt and pepper in a bowl. Stir in chorizo and the remaining ingredients. Pour the mixture into a baking pan and cook for 20-25 minutes on Bake function. Serve sliced.

Prosciutto & Salami Egg Bake

Prep + Cook Time: 35 minutes | Serves: 2

Ingredients

1 beef sausage, chopped
4 slices prosciutto, chopped
3 oz salami, chopped

1 cup grated mozzarella cheese
4 eggs, beaten
½ tsp onion powder

Directions

Preheat Cuisinart on Bake function to 350 F. Whisk the eggs with the onion powder. Brown the sausage in a skillet over medium heat for 2 minutes. Remove to the egg mixture and add in mozzarella cheese, salami, and prosciutto and give it a stir. Pour the egg mixture in a greased baking pan and cook for 20-25 minutes until golden brown on top. Serve.

Cheesy Dutch Pancake

Prep + Cook Time: 30 minutes | Serves: 4

Ingredients

2 tbsp butter, melted
1 cup milk
1 cup all-purpose flour
4 large eggs

2 tsp lemon zest
¼ tsp salt
½ cup cheddar cheese, grated
1 cup sour cream

Directions

Preheat Cuisinart on Bake function to 350 F. In a bowl, beat the milk, eggs, lemon zest, and salt until smooth. Sift the flour into the bowl, whisking constantly to avoid lumps.

Brush the inside of a baking dish with butter and pour in the batter. Bake for 12-14 minutes or lightly golden. Sprinkle the cheese over and return to the oven and bake for 3-5 more minutes until the cheese has melted. Serve hot garnished with sour cream.

Healthy Pecan Granola

Prep + Cook Time: 40 minutes | Serves: 4

Ingredients

3 tbsp extra-virgin olive oil
3 cups rolled oats
1 cup shredded, unsweetened coconut
1 cup pecans, chopped
¼ cup raw sunflower seeds

2 tbsp pumpkin seeds
½ cup honey
¼ tsp ground cinnamon
¼ tsp ground ground cardamom
½ cup sultanas

Directions

Preheat Cuisinart on Bake function to 350 F. Lay wax paper on a baking sheet.

Thoroughly combine the oats, coconut, pecans, sunflower seeds, and pumpkin seeds in a bowl, stirring to mix well. In a separate bowl, mix the honey, olive oil, cinnamon, and cardamon until uniform. Add in the nut mixture and stir until everything is coated. Spread the mixture on the prepared baking sheet. Cook the granola for 30 minutes, stirring once or twice during the cooking time. Remove and stir in sultanas. Allow your granola to cool down. Serve.

Almond & Cinnamon Berry Oat Bars

Prep + Cook Time: 30 minutes | Serves: 6

Ingredients

½ cup canola oil
3 cups rolled oats
½ cup ground almonds
½ cup flour
1 tsp baking powder

1 tsp ground cinnamon
3 eggs, lightly beaten
⅓ cup milk
2 tsp vanilla extract
2 cups mixed berries

Directions

Spray the Cuisinart baking pan with cooking spray. In a bowl, add oats, almonds, flour, baking powder and cinnamon and stir well. In another bowl, whisk eggs, canola oil, milk, and vanilla.

Stir the wet ingredients gently into the oat mixture. Fold in the berries. Pour the mixture in the pan and place in the toaster oven. Cook for 15-20 minutes at 350 F on Bake function until is nice and soft. Let cool and cut into bars to serve.

Cheddar Cheese Hash Browns

Prep + Cook Time: 25 minutes | Serves: 4

Ingredients

4 russet potatoes, peeled, grated
1 brown onion, chopped
2 garlic cloves, chopped
½ cup grated cheddar cheese

1 egg, lightly beaten
Salt and black pepper to taste
2 tbsp thyme, chopped

Directions

In a bowl, mix potatoes, onion, garlic, cheese, egg, salt, black pepper, and thyme. Spray the fryer tray with cooking spray. Press the hash brown mixture into the tray. Cook in the Cuisinart oven for 12-16 minutes at 400 F on Bake function. Shake once halfway through cooking until the hash browns are golden and crispy. Serve.

Caprese Sandwich with Sourdough Bread

Prep + Cook Time: 15 minutes | Serves: 2

Ingredients

4 slices sourdough bread
2 tbsp mayonnaise
2 slices ham
2 lettuce leaves

1 tomato, sliced
2 slices mozzarella cheese
Salt and black pepper to taste

Directions

On a clean board, lay the sourdough slices and spread with mayonnaise. Top 2 of the slices with ham, lettuce, tomato, and mozzarella cheese. Season with salt and pepper.

Top with the remaining two slices to form two sandwiches. Spray with oil and transfer to the fryer basket. Fit in the baking tray and cook in your Cuisinart for 10 minutes at 350 F on Bake function, flipping once halfway through cooking. Serve hot.

Cinnamon Mango Bread

Prep + Cook Time: 40 minutes | Serves: 6

Ingredients

½ cup melted butter
2 eggs, lightly beaten
½ cup brown sugar
2 tbsp icing sugar
1 tsp vanilla extract

1 ripe mango, mashed
1 cup plain flour
½ tsp nutmeg
1 tsp baking powder
½ tsp ground cinnamon

Directions

Spray the Cuisinart baking pan with cooking spray and line with parchment paper. In a bowl, whisk butter, eggs, brown sugar, vanilla, and mango. Sift in flour, baking powder, nutmeg, icing sugar, and cinnamon; stir without overmixing. Pour the batter into the pan and place in the toaster oven. Cook for 25-30 minutes at 360 F on Bake function until a toothpick inserted in the middle comes out clean. Let cool on a wire rack before slicing. Serve.

Creamy Parmesan & Ham Shirred Eggs

Prep + Cook Time: 20 minutes | Serves: 4

Ingredients

4 eggs
2 tbsp heavy cream
4 ham slices
3 tbsp Parmesan cheese, shredded

¼ tsp paprika
Salt and black pepper to taste
2 tsp chopped chives

Directions

Preheat Cuisinart on Bake function to 350 F. Line the bottom of 4 greased ramekins with the ham. Top with heavy cream, salt, and pepper.

Carefully crack the eggs over the cream without breaking the yolks. Cook for 10 minutes until the egg whites are firm. Sprinkle with Parmesan cheese and paprika and bake for 3-4 more minutes until the cheese melts. Garnish with chives and serve.

Baked Chicken with Spinach & Kale Salad

Prep + Cook Time: 20 minutes | Serves: 4

Ingredients

3 tbsp olive oil, divided
2 cups baby spinach leaves
2 cups shredded romaine lettuce
6 large kale leaves, chopped

2 chicken breasts, sliced
1 tsp balsamic vinegar
1 garlic clove, minced
Salt and black pepper to taste

Directions

Place the chicken, 1 tbsp of olive oil, salt, pepper, and garlic in a bowl; toss to combine. Put on a lined Air Fryer pan and cook in your Cuisinart for 14 minutes at 390 F on Bake function.

Place the greens in a large bowl. Add the remaining olive oil and balsamic vinegar. Season with salt and pepper and toss to combine. Top with the chicken and serve.

Pear & Almond Oatmeal

Prep + Cook Time: 45 minutes | Serves: 4

Ingredients

2 tbsp butter, melted
1 cup rolled oats
¾ tsp baking powder
¾ tsp ground ginger
¼ tsp salt
¾ cup milk

¼ cup maple syrup
1 fresh egg
1 tsp vanilla extract
1 pear, peeled and chopped
½ tbsp toasted almond flakes

Directions

Preheat Cuisinart on Bake function to 380 F. Thoroughly combine the oats, baking powder, ginger, and salt in a large bowl. In a separate bowl, add the milk, maple syrup, egg, butter, and vanilla and whisk well. Add the wet mixture to the dry ingredients and mix again to combine.

Stir in the pear. Pour the batter into a greased baking pan and Bake for 35 minutes. When finished, the oatmeal should look firm in the center. Let cool for a few minutes, then divide the oatmeal between individual bowls. Top each serving with almond flakes and serve immediately.

Classic Bacon & Egg English Muffin

Prep + Cook Time: 15 minutes | Serves: 1

Ingredients

1 egg
1 English muffin

2 slices of bacon
Salt and black pepper to taste

Directions

Preheat Cuisinart on Bake function to 395 F. Crack the egg into a ramekin. Place the English muffin, egg ramekin, and bacon in a baking pan. Cook for 9 minutes. Let cool slightly so you can assemble the sandwich. Cut the muffin in half. Slide the egg on one half and season with salt and pepper. Top with the bacon. Cover with the other muffin half. Serve and enjoy!

Asparagus & Mushroom Frittata

Prep + Cook Time: 50 minutes | Serves:4

Ingredients

1 tbsp olive oil

1 cup white mushrooms, chopped

1 shallot, finely chopped

1 garlic clove, minced

4 fresh eggs

½ cup milk

6 asparagus spears, chopped

1 tbsp fresh basil, chopped

Salt and black pepper to taste

¾ cup feta cheese, crumbled

Directions

Preheat your Cuisinart to 350 F on Bake function. Coat a baking pan with olive oil and add in the mushrooms, shallot, asparagus, and garlic. Mix and bake for 5 minutes until soft, shaking the pan halfway through the cooking time. As the veggies are cooking, beat the eggs, milk, basil, salt, and pepper in a bowl and whisk to combine well.

Pour the egg mixture over the vegetables; stir. Sprinkle with feta cheese and cook for 25-30 minutes until fluffy and golden; poke the center with a knife to make sure it's cooked through. Allow to cool off for 5 minutes. Then serve.

Morning Bread Pudding

Prep + Cook Time: 40 minutes | Serves: 4

Ingredients

1 loaf rye bread, cubed

5 eggs

1 cup milk

½ cup diced ham

½ cup shredded Pecorino cheese

1 cup spinach, chopped

Salt and black pepper to taste

Directions

Preheat your Cuisinart to 350 F on Bake function. Lay the bread cubes along the bottom of a greased baking pan, making sure they're evenly distributed. Mix the eggs, milk, ham, cheese, spinach, salt, and pepper in a bowl, then pour the mixture over the bread. Cook for 25-30 minutes or until golden. Poke the center with a knife to be sure it's thoroughly cooked. Allow to cool for a few minutes, then serve.

Breakfast Loaded Sweet Potato Skins

Prep + Cook Time: 75 minutes | Serves: 4

Ingredients

1 tsp olive oil
2 sweet potatoes, scrubbed
½ cup cheddar cheese, shredded
4 eggs
¼ cup heavy cream
1 spring onion, chopped
Salt and black pepper to taste

Directions

Preheat Cuisinart on Toast function to 390 F. Poke holes in the potatoes with a fork and brush them with olive oil. Put the potatoes on the rack and cook for 40 minutes until softened. Let them cool for 5-10 minutes. Once cool, cut the potatoes in half lengthwise.

Use a spoon to remove the innards until you have about ½ inch of potato attached to the skin. Set the potato halves in the frying basket and put in the baking tray.

Add 2 tbsp of cheddar cheese to each, then crack an egg on top. Add a dollop of heavy cream on top of the egg. Sprinkle with spring onion, salt, and pepper. Cook for 15 minutes until the top is lightly browned and golden. Serve warm.

Tomato, Basil & Mozzarella Breakfast

Prep + Cook Time: 15 minutes | Serves: 1

Ingredients

2 slices of bread
4 tomato slices
4 mozzarella cheese slices
½ tbsp chopped basil
Salt and black pepper to taste

Directions

Preheat Cuisinart on Toast function to 350 F. Place the bread slices in the Cuisinart oven and toast for 3-5 minutes. Layer the bread with mozzarella and tomato slices. Season with salt and pepper. Bake for 3-4 minutes until mozzarella is bubbly. Sprinkle with basil and serve.

Parsley Onion & Feta Tart

Prep + Cook Time: 30 minutes | Serves: 4

Ingredients

2 tbsp olive oil
1 cup pounds feta cheese
1 whole onion, chopped
2 tbsp parsley, chopped
1 egg yolk
4 sheets frozen filo pastry

Directions

Cut each of the 4 filo sheets into three equal-sized strips. Brush the strips with olive oil. In a bowl, mix onion, feta, egg yolk, and parsley. Make triangles using the cut strips and add a little bit of the feta mixture on top of each triangle. Place the triangles in a greased baking sheet and cook for 5 minutes at 400 F on Bake function. Serve and enjoy!

Blue Cheese & Leek Crumble

Prep + Cook Time: 40 minutes | Serves: 6

Ingredients

Filling:

2 tbsp butter, softened
1 zucchini, sliced
2 leeks, finely sliced

1 cup blue cheese, crumbled
Salt and black pepper to taste

Topping:

6 tbsp butter, cold and cubed
¾ cup flour

½ cup rolled oats
Salt and pepper to taste

Directions

Preheat Cuisinart on Bake function to 360 F. Mix the zucchini, leeks, butter, salt, and pepper in a baking dish and bake for 5-8 minutes, shaking the dish once or twice. Stir in the blue cheese.

In a bowl, mix the flour, oats, salt, and pepper. Add and rub the butter with your fingers until the mixture becomes crumbled. Sprinkle the crumble topping over the cheese mixture and place the pan in the lower position. Bake for 15-20 minutes until golden brown on top. Remove and allow to cool slightly, then serve.

Giant Strawberry Pancake

Prep + Cook Time: 30 minutes | Serves: 3

Ingredients

2 tbsp butter, melted
3 eggs, beaten
1 cup flour

2 tbsp sugar, powdered
1 cup milk
1 ½ cups fresh strawberries, sliced

Directions

Preheat Cuisinart on Bake function to 350 F. In a bowl, mix flour, milk, eggs, and butter until fully incorporated. Add the mixture to a greased baking pan. Place the pan in your Cuisinart oven and cook for 12-16 minutes until the pancake is fluffy and golden brown. Dust with powdered sugar and arrange the sliced strawberries on top. Serve.

Carrot & Parsnip Patties

Prep + Cook Time: 20 minutes | Serves: 4

Ingredients

1 tbsp olive oil
1 large parsnip, grated
2 carrots, grated
3 eggs, beaten

½ tsp garlic powder
¼ tsp nutmeg
1 cup flour
Salt and black pepper to taste

Directions

In a bowl, combine flour, eggs, parsnip, carrots, nutmeg, and garlic powder. Season with salt and pepper. Form patties out of the mixture. Drizzle the AirFryer basket with olive oil and arrange the patties inside. Fit in the baking tray and cook in your Cuisinart for 15 minutes on Air Fry function at 360 F. Serve with garlic mayo.

Italian Avocado & Cheese Bruschetta

Prep + Cook Time: 15 minutes | Serves: 4

Ingredients

2 tbsp olive oil
1 Italian ciabatta, sliced
2 garlic cloves, halved lengthwise
1 avocado, pitted, peeled and sliced

½ lemon, juiced
1 ball fresh mozzarella cheese, sliced
½ cup black olives, pitted and sliced
5 oz baby spinach

Directions

Preheat Cuisinart on Bake function to 400 F. Rub the ciabatta slices with garlic and drizzle with some olive oil. Toast the bread slices for 5-6 minutes until lightly browned around the edges. Cover the bread with baby spinach and layer the mozzarella and avocado slices on top. Drizzle with lemon juice and remaining olive oil and sprinkle with black olives to serve.

Buttered Apple & Brie Cheese Sandwich

Prep + Cook Time: 10 minutes | Serves: 2

Ingredients

2 tsp butter
4 bread slices

1 apple, thinly sliced
4 brie cheese slices, thinly sliced

Directions

Spread butter on the bread slices. Layer the apple slices on top and cover with another even layer of brie cheese. Cook in your Cuisinart for 5 minutes at 350 F on Bake function. Serve.

Effortless Cheesy Baked Eggs

Prep + Cook Time: 20 minutes | Serves: 4

Ingredients

4 large eggs
1 tsp paprika

Salt and black pepper to taste
¼ cup cottage cheese, crumbled

Directions

Preheat your Cuisinart fryer to 350 F on Bake function. Crack the eggs into 4 greased muffin cups. Sprinkle with salt and pepper. Top with cottage cheese. Put the cups in the Air Fryer tray and bake for 12-15 minutes. Remove and sprinkle with paprika to serve.

Herby Parmesan Bagels

Prep + Cook Time: 15 minutes | Serves: 2

Ingredients

2 tbsp butter, softened
¼ tsp dried basil
¼ tsp dried parsley
½ tsp garlic powder

2 tbsp Parmesan cheese
Salt and black pepper to taste
2 bagels

Directions

Preheat Cuisinart on Bake function to 370 degrees. Cut the bagels in half. Combine the butter, Parmesan cheese, garlic, basil, and parsley in a small bowl. Season with salt and pepper. Spread the mixture onto the bagels. Bake for 5-10 minutes or until golden and bubbly. Serve.

Swiss Cheese Sausage Cakes

Prep + Cook Time: 25 minutes | Serves: 4

Ingredients

1 lb ground Italian sausage
¼ cup Swiss cheese, shredded
¼ cup breadcrumbs
2 tbsp parsley, chopped

1 tsp red pepper flakes
Salt and black pepper to taste
¼ tsp garlic powder
1 egg, beaten

Directions

Preheat Cuisinart on Air Fry function to 350 F. Combine all of the ingredients in a large bowl. Line a baking sheet with parchment paper. Make patties out of the sausage mixture and arrange them on the baking sheet. Cook for 15 minutes, flipping once or until slightly browned. Serve.

Vanilla & Cinnamon Toast

Prep + Cook Time: 20 minutes | Serves: 6

Ingredients

12 bread slices
½ cup sugar
1 ½ tsp cinnamon

1 ½ butter stick, softened
1 tsp vanilla extract

Directions

Preheat Cuisinart on Toast function to 360 F. Place all ingredients, except the bread, in a bowl and stir to combine completely. Spread the mixture onto the bread slices. Place the bread slices in the toaster oven. Cook for 8-10 minutes or until golden brown. Serve sliced diagonally.

Porridge with Honey & Peanut Butter

Prep + Cook Time: 15 minutes | Serves: 4

Ingredients

2 cups steel-cut oats
1 cup flax seeds
1 tbsp peanut butter

1 tbsp butter
4 cups milk
4 tbsp honey

Directions

Preheat Cuisinart on Bake function to 390 F. Combine all of the ingredients in an ovenproof bowl. Place in a baking pan and cook for 7 minutes. Stir and serve.

Vanilla Brownie Squares

Prep + Cook Time: 40 minutes | Serves: 2

Ingredients

2 tbsp safflower oil
1 whole egg, beaten
¼ cup chocolate chips
2 tbsp white sugar

⅓ cup flour
1 tsp vanilla extract
¼ cup cocoa powder

Directions

Preheat Cuisinart on Bake function to 360 F. In a bowl, mix the egg, sugar, oil, and vanilla. In another bowl, mix cocoa powder and flour. Add the flour mixture to the vanilla mixture and stir until fully incorporated. Pour the mixture into a greased baking pan and sprinkle chocolate chips on top. Cook for 25-30 minutes. Chill and cut into squares to serve.

APPETIZERS & SIDE DISHES

Perfect Crispy Potatoes

Prep + Cook Time: 35 minutes | Serves: 4

Ingredients

2 tbsp olive oil
1 ½ pounds potatoes, halved
3 garlic cloves, grated
1 tbsp minced fresh rosemary
Salt and black pepper to taste

Directions

In a bowl, mix potatoes, oil, garlic, rosemary, salt, and pepper until well-coated. Arrange the potatoes on the basket and fit in the baking tray. Cook in the Cuisinart at 360 F on Air Fry function for 20-25 minutes, shaking twice until crispy on the outside and tender on the inside. Serve.

Egg Roll Wrapped with Cabbage & Prawns

Prep + Cook Time: 50 minutes | Serves: 4

Ingredients

2 tbsp vegetable oil
1 tbsp sesame oil
1-inch piece fresh ginger, grated
1 tbsp minced garlic
1 carrot, cut into strips
¼ cup chicken broth
2 tbsp reduced-sodium soy sauce
1 tbsp sugar
1 cup shredded Napa cabbage
8 cooked prawns, chopped
1 egg
8 egg roll wrappers

Directions

Heat the vegetable oil in a skillet over medium heat and sauté ginger and garlic for 40 seconds until fragrant. Stir in carrot and cook for another 2 minutes. Pour in chicken broth, soy sauce, and sugar and bring to a boil. Add in cabbage and let simmer until softened, about 4 minutes. Remove skillet from the heat and stir in sesame oil. Let cool for 15 minutes.

Strain the cabbage mixture and fold in the prawns. Whisk the egg in a small bowl. Fill each egg roll wrapper with prawn mixture, arranging the mixture just below the center of the wrapper. Fold the bottom part over the filling and tuck under. Fold in both sides and tightly roll-up.

Use the whisked egg to seal the wrapper. Repeat until all egg rolls are ready. Place the rolls into a greased frying basket, spray them with oil and fit in the baking tray. Cook in your Cuisinart for 12 minutes at 370 F on Air Fry function, turning once halfway through. Serve.

Homemade Tortilla Chips

Prep + Cook Time: 25 minutes | Serves: 4

Ingredients

1 cup flour

Salt and black pepper to taste

1 tbsp golden flaxseed meal

2 cups shredded Cheddar cheese

Directions

Melt cheddar cheese in the microwave for 1 minute. Add flour, salt, flaxseed meal, and pepper. Mix well with a fork. On a board, place the dough and knead it with your hands while warm until the ingredients are well combined. Divide the dough into 2 and with a rolling pin, roll them out flat into 2 rectangles. Use a pastry cutter to cut out triangle-shaped pieces.

Line them in one layer on the fryer basket and spray with cooking spray. Fit in the baking tray and cook in the Cuisinart for 10 minutes on Air Fry function at 400 F. Serve with cheese dip.

Crunchy Cheese & Cauliflower Twists

Prep + Cook Time: 30 minutes | Serves: 3

Ingredients

2 cups cauliflower florets, cooked and mashed

1 egg

1 cup oats

1 red onion, diced

1 tsp mustard

5 oz cheddar cheese, shredded

Salt and black pepper to taste

Directions

Preheat Cuisinart on Air Fry function to 350 F. Place the oats in a food processor and pulse until you obtain a breadcrumb consistency.

Place the cauliflower in a large bowl. Add in the rest of the ingredients and mix to combine. Take a little bit of the mixture and twist it into a straw.

Place onto a lined baking tray and repeat the process with the rest of the mixture. Cook for 10 minutes, turn over, and cook for an additional 10 minutes. Serve.

Southern Sweet Pickle Chips

Prep + Cook Time: 35 minutes | Serves: 3

Ingredients

36 sweet pickle chips

1 cup buttermilk

3 tbsp smoked paprika

2 cups flour

¼ cup cornmeal

Salt and black pepper to taste

Directions

Preheat Cuisinart on Air Fryer function to 400 F. In a bowl, mix flour, smoked paprika, pepper, salt, and cornmeal. Place the pickles in the buttermilk and let sit for 5 minutes. Remove and shake off. Dip the pickles into the spice mixture and place them in the greased frying basket. Fit in the baking tray and cook for 15-20 minutes, shaking halfway through. Serve warm.

Mixed Nuts with Cinnamon

Prep + Cook Time: 30 minutes | Serves: 4

Ingredients

½ cup pecans
½ cup walnuts
½ cup almonds
2 tbsp egg whites

A pinch of cayenne pepper
2 tbsp sugar
2 tsp cinnamon

Directions

Add the cayenne pepper, sugar, and cinnamon to a bowl and mix well; set aside. In another bowl, combine the pecans, walnuts, almonds, and egg whites. Add the spice mixture to the nuts and give it a good mix. Lightly grease the baking tray with cooking spray.

Pour in the nuts and cook for 10 minutes in your Cuisinart on Bake function at 350 F. Shake and cook for further for 10 minutes. Pour the nuts into a bowl. Let cool before serving.

Sesame Garlic Chicken Wings

Prep + Cook Time: 35 minutes + chilling time| Serves: 4

Ingredients

1 pound chicken wings
1 cup soy sauce
½ cup brown sugar
½ cup apple cider vinegar
2 tbsp fresh ginger, minced

2 tbsp fresh garlic, minced
1 tsp finely ground black pepper
2 tbsp cornstarch
2 tbsp cold water
1 tsp sesame seeds

Directions

In a bowl, mix the chicken wings with a half cup of soy sauce. Refrigerate for 20 minutes, drain, and pat dry. Arrange the wings on the fryer basket and fit in the baking tray. Cook for 20 minutes at 380 F on Air Fry function, turning once halfway through.

In a skillet over medium heat, stir sugar, remaining soy sauce, vinegar, ginger, garlic, and pepper. Cook until the sauce has reduced slightly. Dissolve cornstarch in cold water and stir in the sauce; cook until it thickens, 2 minutes. Pour the sauce over wings and sprinkle with sesame seeds.

Crispy Zucchini Strips

Prep + Cook Time: 20 minutes | Serves: 4

Ingredients

1 lb zucchini, cut into strips
1 cup flour
2 fresh eggs

1 ½ cups breadcrumbs
½ cup Pecorino cheese, grated
Salt and black pepper to taste

Directions

Preheat Cuisinart on Air Fry function to 350 F. Whisk the eggs in a bowl with salt and pepper. In a separate bowl, mix together the breadcrumbs and Pecorino cheese. Put the frying basket on a baking sheet and spritz with cooking spray.

Coat the zucchini strips with flour, then dip in the egg mix. Lastly, roll them in the crumbs. Spritz all sides of the strips with cooking spray, then arrange them on the basket in an even layer. Air fry for 5 minutes, flip, then air fry for 5 more minutes until golden and crispy. Serve warm.

Cheesy Sticks with Thai Sauce

Prep + Cook Time: 20 minutes + freezing time| Serves: 4

Ingredients

12 mozzarella string cheese
2 cups breadcrumbs
3 eggs

1 cup sweet Thai sauce
4 tbsp skimmed milk

Directions

Pour the crumbs into a bowl. Crack the eggs into another bowl and beat with the milk. One after the other, dip each cheese stick in the egg mixture, in the crumbs, then egg mixture again, and finally in the crumbs back. Place the cheese sticks in a cookie sheet and freeze for 2 hours.

Preheat your Cuisinart on Air Fry function to 380 F. Arrange the sticks on the frying basket without overcrowding. Fit in the baking tray and cook for 8 minutes, flipping halfway through cooking until browned. Serve with the sweet Thai sauce.

Grandma's Apple Cinnamon Chips

Prep + Cook Time: 20 minutes | Serves: 2

Ingredients

1 tsp sugar
1 tsp salt
1 whole apple, sliced

½ tsp cinnamon
Confectioners' sugar for serving

Directions

Preheat your Cuisinart to 400 F on Bake function. In a bowl, mix cinnamon, salt, and sugar. Add in the apple slices and toss to coat. Place the prepared apple slices in the greased fryer basket and fit in the cooking tray. Cook for 10 minutes, flipping once. Dust with sugar and serve.

Bacon-Wrapped Jalapeño Popper Stuffed Chicken

Prep + Cook Time: 30 minutes | Serves: 4

Ingredients

8 Jalapeno peppers, halved and seeded
2 chicken breasts, butterflied and halved
6 oz cream cheese
6 oz Cheddar cheese

12 slices bacon
1 cup breadcrumbs
Salt and black pepper to taste
2 eggs

Directions

Season the chicken with salt and pepper. In a bowl, add cream and cheddar cheeses and mix well. Spoon the cheese mixture into the jalapeno halves to the brim. Press the jalapeños halves back together. Place a stuffed jalapeño on each chicken half and fold them to close. Wrap each stuffed chicken breast with 3 bacon slices and secure the ends with toothpicks.

Preheat Cuisinart on Air Fry function to 350 F. Add the eggs to a bowl and pour the breadcrumbs into another bowl. Take each wrapped jalapeño and dip it into the eggs and then in the breadcrumbs. Working in batches, arrange the breaded peppers on the greased fryer basket, fit in the baking tray, and cook for 7 minutes. Turn and cook further for 4 minutes.

Once ready, remove them onto a paper towel-lined plate. Repeat the cooking process for the remaining jalapenos. Serve with a sweet dip for an enhanced taste.

Cheese & Ham Eggplant Boats

Prep + Cook Time: 20 minutes | Serves: 2

Ingredients

1 eggplant
4 ham slices, chopped
1 cup shredded mozzarella cheese

1 tsp dried parsley
Salt and black pepper to taste

Directions

Preheat Cuisinart on Bake function to 400 F. Cut the eggplant lengthwise in half and scoop some flesh out. Season with salt and pepper. Divide half of the mozzarella cheese between the eggplant halves and cover with the ham slices. Top with the remaining mozzarella cheese, sprinkle with parsley, and cook for 14-16 minutes. Serve warm.

Maple Shrimp with Coconut

Prep + Cook Time: 20 minutes | Serves: 3

Ingredients

1 lb jumbo shrimp, peeled and deveined
¾ cup shredded coconut
1 tbsp maple syrup

½ cup breadcrumbs
⅓ cup cornstarch
½ cup milk

Directions

Pour the cornstarch in a zipper bag, add shrimp, zip the bag up, and shake vigorously to coat. Mix the maple syrup and milk in a bowl and set aside.

In a separate bowl, mix the breadcrumbs and shredded coconut. Open the zipper bag and remove the shrimp, shaking off excess starch. Dip the shrimp in the milk mixture and then in the crumb mixture while pressing loosely to trap enough crumbs and coconut.

Place in the basket without overcrowding and fit in the baking tray. Cook for 10-12 minutes at 350 F on Air Fry function, flipping once halfway through until golden brown. Serve warm.

Cheesy Crisps

Prep + Cook Time: 20 minutes | Serves: 3

Ingredients

3 tsp butter
4 tbsp grated cheddar cheese + extra for rolling
1 cup flour + extra for kneading

¼ tsp chili powder
½ tsp baking powder
A pinch of salt

Directions

In a bowl, add the cheddar cheese, flour, baking powder, chili powder, butter, and salt and mix until the mixture becomes crusty. Add some drops of water and mix well to get a dough.

Transfer the dough to a clean and lightly floured working surface and knead it for a while. Using a rolling pin, roll the dough out into a thin sheet. With a pastry cutter, cut the dough into your desired lings' shape. Add the cheese lings to the greased baking tray and cook for 8 minutes at 350 F on Air Fry function, flipping once halfway through. Serve.

Delicious Chicken Wings with Alfredo Sauce

Prep + Cook Time: 60 minutes | Serves: 4

Ingredients

1 ½ pounds chicken wings
Salt and black pepper to taste

½ cup Alfredo sauce

Directions

Preheat Cuisinart on Air Fry function to 370 F. Season the wings with salt and pepper. Arrange them on the greased basket without touching. Fit in the baking tray and cook for 20 minutes until no longer pink in the center. Work in batches if needed. Increase the heat to 390 F and cook for 5 minutes more. Remove to a large bowl and drizzle with the Alfredo sauce. Serve.

Golden Parmesan Chicken Nuggets

Prep + Cook Time: 25 minutes | Serves: 4

Ingredients

2 tbsp olive oil

1 lb chicken breasts, cubed

Salt and black pepper to taste

5 tbsp plain breadcrumbs

2 tbsp panko breadcrumbs

2 tbsp grated Parmesan cheese

Directions

Preheat Cuisinart on Air Fry function to 380 F. Season the chicken with salt and pepper; set aside. In a bowl, mix the breadcrumbs and Parmesan cheese.

Brush the chicken pieces with olive oil, dip into the breadcrumb mixture, and transfer to the fryer basket. Fit in the baking tray and lightly spray chicken with cooking spray. Cook for 10-14 minutes until golden brown on the outside and no more pink on the inside, flipping once halfway through. Serve warm.

Fried Green Tomatoes

Prep + Cook Time: 20 minutes | Serves: 4

Ingredients

4 large green tomatoes

2 eggs

½ cup milk

½ cup cornmeal

1 cup flour

Salt and black pepper to taste

1 ½ cups breadcrumbs

½ tsp dried oregano

Directions

Preheat Cuisinart on Air Fry function to 400 F. Cut the tomatoes into ¼-inch thick slices; discard the ends. Beat the eggs with milk and salt in a bowl. Mix together the cornmeal, breadcrumbs, salt, pepper, and oregano in a second bowl. Pour the flour on a plate.

Dredge the tomato slices in the flour first, then into the egg mixture, and then coat the slices into the cornmeal mixture; shake off. Place the tomato slices in the greased baking sheet. Spritz with cooking spray. Cook for 8-10 minutes, flipping halfway through the cooking time until golden brown. Serve immediately.

Pancetta-Wrapped Goat Cheese Bombs

Prep + Cook Time: 20 minutes | Serves: 6

Ingredients

16 oz soft goat cheese
2 tbsp fresh rosemary, finely chopped
1 cup almonds, chopped into small pieces

Salt and black pepper to taste
15 dried plums, chopped
15 pancetta slices

Directions

Line the Cuisinart Air Fryer tray with parchment paper. In a bowl, add goat cheese, rosemary, almonds, salt, pepper, and plums; stir well. Roll into balls and wrap with pancetta slices. Arrange the bombs on the tray and cook for 10 minutes at 400 F. Let cool before serving.

Mini Salmon Quiches

Prep + Cook Time: 20 minutes | Serves: 15

Ingredients

15 mini tart cases
4 eggs, lightly beaten
½ cup heavy cream

3 oz smoked salmon, chopped
6 oz feta cheese, crumbled
2 tsp fresh dill, chopped

Directions

Mix together eggs and heavy cream in a bowl. Arrange the tarts on a greased baking tray. Fill them with the egg mixture, about halfway up the side and top with salmon and feta cheese. Cook in your Cuisinart for 10 minutes at 360 F on Bake function, regularly checking to avoid overcooking. Sprinkle with dill and serve chilled.

Allspice Chicken Wings

Prep + Cook Time: 35 minutes | Serves: 4

Ingredients

½ tsp celery salt
½ tsp bay leaf powder
½ tsp ground black pepper
½ tsp paprika

¼ tsp dry mustard
¼ tsp cayenne pepper
¼ tsp allspice
2 pounds chicken wings

Directions

Preheat your Cuisinart to 340 F on Air Fry function. In a bowl, mix celery salt, bay leaf powder, black pepper, paprika, dry mustard, cayenne pepper, and allspice. Coat the wings thoroughly with the mixture.

Arrange the wings in an even layer on the greased frying basket and fit in the baking tray. Cook the chicken until no longer pink around the bone, about 20-22 minutes. Then, increase the temperature to 380 F and cook for 6 minutes more until crispy on the outside. Serve warm.

Easy Scalloped Red Potatoes

Prep + Cook Time: 60 minutes | Serves: 4

Ingredients

2 tbsp butter
1 pound red potatoes
1 small onion, finely chopped
½ tsp cayenne pepper
½ tsp dried oregano

2 tbsp flour
1 cup whole milk
½ cup vegetable broth
¼ tsp ground nutmeg
Salt and black pepper to taste

Directions

Preheat Cuisinart on Air Fry function to 360 F. Peel and cut the potatoes into ¼ inch thick slices. Melt the butter in a skillet over medium heat. Stir-fry the onion for 3 minutes until tender. Stir in the flour for 30-40 seconds. Pour in the milk and broth and simmer for 3-4 minutes, stirring constantly, until it thickens. Take the pan off the burner and stir in the cayenne pepper, oregano, nutmeg, salt, and pepper; set aside.

Place a third of the potato slices in a greased baking pan; pour a third of the sauce over them. Repeat until all the potatoes are used, ending with the sauce. Cover with aluminum foil and cook for 20-25 minutes. Take the foil off and bake for 10-15 minutes until golden and fork-tender.

Crispy Cod Fingers

Prep + Cook Time: 20 minutes | Serves: 4

Ingredients

2 cups flour
Salt and black pepper to taste
1 tsp seafood seasoning
2 whole eggs, beaten
1 cup cornmeal

1 pound cod fillets, cut into fingers
2 tbsp milk
1 cup breadcrumbs
1 lemon, cut into wedges

Directions

Preheat Cuisinart on Air Fryer function to 400 F. In a bowl, mix beaten eggs with milk. In a separate bowl, combine flour, cornmeal, and seafood seasoning. In a third bowl, stir the breadcrumbs with salt and pepper. Dip cod fingers in the flour mixture, followed by the egg mixture, and finally coat with breadcrumbs. Place the fingers in your fryer basket and fit in the baking tray. Cook for 10 minutes until golden brown, shaking once. Serve with lemon wedges.

Heby Cornbread

Prep + Cook Time: 35 minutes | Serves: 4

Ingredients

¼ cup salted butter, melted
¼ tsp dried oregano
¼ tsp dried basil
¼ tsp dried sage
¾ cup flour

¾ cup yellow cornmeal
2 tsp baking powder
½ tsp salt
¾ cup buttermilk
1 large egg

Directions

Preheat Cuisinart on Bake function to 400 F. Add the flour, cornmeal, oregano, basil, sage, baking powder, and salt to a bowl and stir until combined. In a separate bowl, whisk the egg, buttermilk, and melted butter until blended. Add the wet mixture to the dry ingredients and gently stir again to combine. Pour the batter into a greased baking pan and bake for 20-25 minutes until the cornbread is crisp around the edges; poke the center with a knife to make sure it's cooked thoroughly. Let the cornbread cool on a wire rack. Cut into wedges and serve.

Two-Cheese Stuffed Mushrooms

Prep + Cook Time: 25 minutes | Serves: 4

Ingredients

2 tbsp olive oil
8 button mushrooms, stalks removed
2 garlic cloves, minced
1 cup cream cheese

1 cup grated Grana Padano cheese
2 tbsp chives, chopped
¼ cup breadcrumbs
Salt and black pepper to taste

Directions

Preheat Cuisinart on Bake function to 360 F. Brush the mushrooms with olive oil and arrange them onto the Cuisinart Air Fryer baking tray. In a bowl, mix the garlic, cream cheese, Grana Padano cheese, breadcrumbs, salt, and pepper. Spoon the mixture into the mushroom caps. Cook in the Cuisinart for 14-18 minutes until the cheese has melted. Serve topped with chives.

Louisiana Hot Chicken Wings

Prep + Cook Time: 25 minutes | Serves: 3

Ingredients

⅓ cup butter
15 chicken wings
Salt and black pepper to taste

½ tbsp vinegar
1 cup Louisiana hot sauce

Directions

Preheat Cuisinart on Air Fry function to 360 F. Season the wings with salt and pepper. Add them to the greased basket and fit in the baking tray. Cook for 15 minutes. Toss every 5 minutes. Once ready, remove them to a bowl. Melt the butter in a saucepan over low heat.

Add in the vinegar and hot sauce. Stir and cook for a minute. Turn the heat off. Pour the sauce over the chicken. Toss to coat thoroughly. Transfer the chicken to a serving platter. Serve with a side of celery strips and blue cheese dressing.

Cinnamon Eggplant Cakes

Prep + Cook Time: 25 minutes | Serves: 4

Ingredients

2 tbsp butter, melted
1 ½ cups flour
1 tsp cinnamon
3 eggs
2 tsp baking powder
2 tbsp sugar

1 cup milk
1 tbsp yogurt
½ cup shredded eggplants
A pinch of salt
2 tbsp cream cheese

Directions

Preheat Cuisinart on Air Fry function to 350 F. In a bowl, whisk the eggs and the sugar, salt, cinnamon, cream cheese, flour, and baking powder. In another bowl, combine all of the liquid ingredients. Gently combine the dry and liquid mixtures; stir in eggplants.

Line the muffin tins and pour the batter inside; cook for 12 minutes. Check with a toothpick: you may need to cook them for an additional 2 to 3 minutes. Serve chilled.

Prosciutto & Mozzarella Crostini

Prep + Cook Time: 15 minutes | Serves: 3

Ingredients

1 tbsp olive oil
½ cup finely chopped tomatoes
3 oz chopped mozzarella

3 prosciutto slices, chopped
1 tsp dried basil
9 French bread slices

Directions

Preheat Cuisinart on Toast function to 350 F. Place the bread slices in the toaster oven and toast for 5 minutes. Top the bread with tomatoes, prosciutto, and mozzarella.

Sprinkle the basil over the mozzarella. Drizzle with olive oil. Return to oven and cook for 1 more minute, enough to become melty and warm.

Lime Corn with Feta

Prep + Cook Time: 20 minutes | Serves: 2

Ingredients

2 ears of corn
Juice of 2 small limes

2 tsp paprika
4 oz feta cheese, grated

Directions

Preheat Cuisinart on Air Fry function to 370 F. Peel the corn and remove the silk. Place the corn on the baking pan and cook for 15 minutes. Squeeze the juice of 1 lime on top of each ear of corn. Top with feta cheese and paprika. Serve and enjoy!

Mustardy Green Beans

Prep + Cook Time: 15 minutes | Serves: 4

Ingredients:

4 tbsp olive oil
1 pound green beans, stems trimmed
Salt to taste

2 tbsp Dijon mustard
2 tbsp honey
1 tbsp lemon juice

Directions

Preheat Cuisinart on Air Fry function to 350 F. Drizzle some olive oil over the green beans and season with salt. Put the frying basket on the baking tray and toss the beans inside it. Fry for 8 minutes, shaking once. The beans should be aromatic and golden.

In a bowl, whisk the remaining olive oil, mustard, honey, lemon juice, and salt. Put the beans on a plate and pour the dressing over to serve.

Patatas Panaderas (Potato Chips)

Prep + Cook Time: 40 minutes + marinating time | Serves: 3

Ingredients

¼ cup olive oil
3 whole potatoes, cut into thin slices
1 garlic clove, minced

½ tsp dried rosemary
Salt to taste

Directions

Preheat Cuisinart on Air Fry function to 390 F. In a bowl, whisk the olive oil, garlic, and salt. Stir in the potatoes. Allow sitting for 10 minutes. Lay the potato slices onto the frying basket and fit in the baking tray. Cook for 20-25 minutes. After 10-12 minutes, give the chips a turn. When ready, sprinkle with rosemary and serve.

Crispy Calamari Rings

Prep + Cook Time: 20 minutes + chilling time| Serves: 4

Ingredients

1 lb calamari (squid), cut in rings
¼ cup flour

2 large eggs, beaten
1 cup breadcrumbs

Directions

Coat the calamari rings with the flour and dip them in the eggs. Then, dip in the breadcrumbs. Refrigerate for 30 minutes. Remove and arrange on the fryer basket; spritz with cooking spray. Fit in the baking tray and cook for 10-12 minutes at 380 F on Air Fry function, flipping once. Serve with garlic mayo and lemon wedges if desired.

Herb Roasted Baby Potatoes

Prep + Cook Time: 30 minutes | Serves: 4

Ingredients

2 tbsp olive oil
1 pound baby potatoes, scrubbed and halved
1 tsp garlic, minced
1 tbsp fresh parsley, chopped

1 tbsp fresh oregano, chopped
1 tbsp fresh basil, chopped
Salt and black pepper to taste

Directions

Preheat Cuisinart on Air Fry function to 390 F. Add the baby potatoes, olive oil, garlic, parsley, oregano, basil, salt, and black pepper to a bowl and toss to coat. Put the frying basket on the baking sheet, then lay the potatoes in a single layer. Bake for 20-25 minutes, shaking once, or until the potatoes are fork-tender and golden brown on top. Serve warm.

Herby Crispy Chickpeas

Prep + Cook Time: 20 minutes | Serves: 4

Ingredients

2 tbsp olive oil
2 (14.5-ounce) cans chickpeas, rinsed
1 tsp dried rosemary

½ tsp dried thyme
¼ tsp dried sage
¼ tsp salt

Directions

In a bowl, mix together chickpeas, oil, rosemary, thyme, sage, and salt. Transfer to the Cuisinart Air Fryer baking dish and spread them in an even layer. Cook for 15 minutes at 380 F on Bake function, shaking once until lightly browned. Serve immediately.

Thyme Carrot Cookies

Prep + Cook Time: 30 minutes | Serves: 6

Ingredients

2 tbsp olive oil
5 carrots, shredded
¼ tsp salt
½ cup flour

½ cup oats
1 tsp baking powder
1 whole egg, beaten
1 tbsp thyme

Directions

Preheat Cuisinart on Air Fryer function to 360 F. Sift the flour, salt, and baking powder in a large bowl; stir in the oats. In a separate bowl, beat the egg and oil until combined. Add the carrots, salt, and thyme; mix. Add the wet mixture to the dry ingredients and mix again to combine.

Form the batter into cookie shapes. Place in your Air Fryer baking tray and cook for 14-16 minutes or until puffed and golden. Leave to cool for 5 mins on a wire rack. Serve and enjoy!

Golden Onion Rings

Prep + Cook Time: 20 minutes | Serves: 4

Ingredients

2 sweet onions
½ cup buttermilk
⅓ cup all-purpose flour
½ tsp baking soda

2 eggs
Salt and black pepper to taste
½ tsp dried thyme

Directions

Preheat Cuisinart on Air Fry function to 370 F. Beat the eggs and buttermilk in a bowl until well combined. Sift the flour and baking soda in another bowl. Gradually pour in the egg mixture, whisking constantly until a smooth batter forms.

Peel and slice the onions into ½-inch rings. Season with salt, pepper, and thyme. Line a baking sheet with parchment paper. Dip the rings in the batter. Place them onto the greased basket and then into the baking tray. Cook for 8-12 minutes, flipping once until crispy. Serve immediately.

Pineapple Pork Ribs

Prep + Cook Time: 20 minutes | Serves: 4

Ingredients

2 lb cut spareribs
7 oz salad dressing

1 (5-oz) can pineapple juice
Salt and black pepper to taste

Directions

Preheat your Cuisinart to 390 F on Bake function. Sprinkle the ribs with salt and pepper and place them in a greased baking dish. Cook for 15 minutes. Prepare the sauce by combining the salad dressing and the pineapple juice. Serve the ribs drizzled with the sauce.

Spicy-Sweet Roasted Nuts & Seeds

Prep + Cook Time: 30 minutes | Serves: 4

Ingredients

1 cup raw almonds
1 cup raw cashews
1 cup raw walnut halves
1 tbsp sunflower seeds
1 tbsp pumpkin seeds
1 large egg white

½ tsp dried thyme
¼ cup sugar
½ tsp chili powder
½ tsp paprika
¼ tsp ground cinnamon

Directions

Preheat Cuisinart on Air Fry function to 320 F. Put the egg white and 1 tbsp of water in a bowl, then whisk until frothy. Toss the nuts and seeds in the mix and shake until well-coated. Put the thyme, sugar, chili powder, paprika, and cinnamon in a bowl and mix well.

Add this mix to the nuts and seeds and stir to combine. Put the frying basket on the baking tray. Add the nuts and seeds in a single layer and air fry for 20 minutes. Shake the basket at the 10-minute mark. The nuts should be golden and dry. Serve chilled.

Spicy Pumpkin-Ham Fritters

Prep + Cook Time: 20 minutes | Serves: 4

Ingredients

1 oz ham, chopped
1 cup dry pancake mix
1 egg
2 tbsp canned puree pumpkin
1 oz cheddar, shredded

½ tsp chili powder
3 tbsp flour
1 oz beer
2 tbsp scallions, chopped

Directions

Preheat Cuisinart on Air Fry function to 370 F. In a bowl, combine the pancake mix and chili powder. Mix in the egg, pumpkin puree, beer, shredded cheddar, ham, and scallions.

Form balls and roll them in the flour. Arrange the balls on the basket and fit in the baking tray. Cook for 8 minutes. Drain on paper towels before serving.

Savory Parsley Crab Cakes

Prep + Cook Time: 20 minutes | Serves: 6

Ingredients

1 tbsp olive oil
1 lb crab meat, shredded
2 eggs, beaten
½ cup breadcrumbs
⅓ cup finely chopped green onions

¼ cup parsley, chopped
1 tbsp mayonnaise
1 tsp sweet chili sauce
½ tsp paprika
Salt and black pepper to taste

Directions

In a bowl, add crab meat, eggs, breadcrumbs, green onion, parsley, mayo, chili sauce, paprika, salt, and black pepper; mix well with your hands. Shape into 6 cakes and grease them lightly with olive oil. Arrange them on the fryer basket without overcrowding. Fit in the baking tray and cook for 8-10 minutes at 400 F on Air Fry function, turning once halfway through.

Homemade Cheesy Sticks

Prep + Cook Time: 15 minutes | Serves: 6

Ingredients

2 tbsp butter, melted
6 (6 oz) bread cheese

2 cups panko crumbs

Directions

With a knife, cut the cheese into equal-sized sticks. Brush each stick with butter and dip into panko crumbs. Arrange the sticks in a single layer on the basket. Fit in the baking tray and cook in the Cuisinart at 390 F for 10 minutes on Air Fry function. Flip halfway through. Serve warm.

Simple Teriyaki Chicken Thighs

Prep + Cook Time: 30 minutes + marinating time| Serves: 2

Ingredients

1 pound chicken thighs
½ cup Teriyaki sauce

1 lime, cut into wedges
2 tbsp chopped cilantro, chopped

Directions

Place the chicken in a bowl and pour over the Teriyaki sauce. Let it sit for 30 minutes. Preheat Cuisinart on Bake function to 350 F. Remove the thighs from the marinade and arrange them, skin side down, on the greased fryer basket; fit in the baking tray. Cook until golden brown, about 20 minutes. Sprinkle with cilantro and serve with lime wedges.

Traditional French Fries

Prep + Cook Time: 30 minutes | Serves: 2

Ingredients

2 tbsp olive oil

2 russet potatoes, cut into strips

Salt and black pepper to taste

Directions

Spray the fryer basket with cooking spray. In a bowl, toss the strips with olive oil until well-coated and season with salt and pepper. Arrange on the basket and fit in the baking tray. Cook in your Cuisinart for 20-25 minutes at 400 F on Air Fry function, turning once halfway through. Check for crispiness and serve immediately with garlic aioli, ketchup, or crumbled cheese.

Harissa Beef Kebab

Prep + Cook Time: 25 minutes + chilling time| Serves: 3

Ingredients

1 lb ground beef

3 tbsp sugar

A pinch of garlic powder

A pinch of harissa powder

Salt to taste

1 tsp liquid smoke

Directions

Place beef, sugar, garlic powder, harissa, salt, and liquid smoke in a bowl. Mix well. Mold out 4 sausage shapes with your hands, place them on a plate, and refrigerate for 30 minutes.

Preheat Cuisinart on Air Fry function to 360 F. Remove and cook in the Cuisinart oven for 10 minutes. Flip and continue cooking for another 5 minutes until browned. Serve immediately.

Simple Chicken Breasts with Tomatoes

Prep + Cook Time: 30 minutes | Serves: 4

Ingredients

4 boneless, skinless chicken breasts

Salt and black pepper to taste

1 tsp garlic powder

2 medium Roma tomatoes, halved

Directions

Spray the breasts and the fryer basket with cooking spray. Rub chicken with salt, garlic powder, and black pepper. Arrange the breasts on the basket. Fit in the baking pan and cook in your Cuisinart for 10 minutes at 360 F on Bake function. Flip the chicken and add the tomatoes. Sprinkle them with salt and spritz with cooking spray; continue cooking for 8-10 minutes until the chicken is nice and crispy and the tomatoes are tender. Slice the breasts and serve warm.

Paprika Cabbage Wedges with Parmesan

Prep + Cook Time: 30 minutes | Serves: 4

Ingredients

4 tbsp butter, melted
½ head of cabbage, cut into 4 wedges
2 cups Parmesan cheese, grated

Salt and black pepper to taste
1 tsp smoked paprika

Directions

Preheat Cuisinart on Air Fry function to 330 F. Line a baking sheet with parchment paper. Brush the cabbage wedges with butter. Season with salt and pepper.

Coat cabbage with Parmesan cheese and arrange on the baking pan; sprinkle with paprika. Cook for 15 minutes, flip, and cook for an additional 10 minutes. Serve with yogurt dip if desired.

Holiday Pumpkin Wedges

Prep + Cook Time: 35 minutes | Serves: 3

Ingredients

½ pumpkin, cut into wedges
½ tbsp paprika
1 lime, squeezed

1 tbsp balsamic vinegar
Salt and black pepper to taste
1 tsp turmeric

Directions

Preheat Cuisinart on Air Fry function to 360 F. Place the pumpkin wedges in your Air Fryer baking tray and cook for 20 minutes, flipping once. In a bowl, mix lime juice, vinegar, turmeric, salt, pepper, and paprika. Pour the mixture over the pumpkin and cook for 5 more minutes.

Ham Rolls with Vegetables & Walnuts

Prep + Cook Time: 20 minutes | Serves: 4

Ingredients

2 tbsp olive oil
8 ham slices
2 carrots, chopped
2 oz walnuts, finely chopped
1 zucchini, chopped

1 garlic clove, minced
1 tbsp ginger powder
¼ cup basil leaves, finely chopped
Salt and black pepper to taste

Directions

Heat the olive oil in a pan over medium heat and add the zucchini, carrots, garlic, ginger, black pepper, and salt; stir-fry for 5 minutes. Add the basil and walnuts and keep stirring.

Divide the mixture between the ham slices. Fold the edges above the filling and roll in. Cook the rolls in the preheated Cuisinart for 8 minutes at 300 F on Bake function. Serve warm.

Potato Chips with Lemony Dip

Prep + Cook Time: 35 minutes | Serves: 4

Ingredients

3 tbsp olive oil
1 lb russet potatoes, sliced
1 cup sour cream

2 scallions, white part minced
½ tsp lemon juice
Salt and black pepper to taste

Directions

Preheat Cuisinart on Air Fry function to 350 F. Place the potatoes into the AirFryer basket Cuisinart and fit in the baking tray. Cook for 20-25 minutes, flipping once. Season with salt and pepper. Mix sour cream, olive oil, scallions, lemon juice, salt, and pepper and serve with chips.

Bok Choy Crisps

Prep + Cook Time: 15 minutes | Serves: 2

Ingredients

2 tbsp olive oil
4 cups packed bok choy
1 tsp Old bay seasoning

1 tbsp yeast flakes
Sea salt to taste

Directions

In a bowl, mix oil, bok choy, yeast flakes, and old bay seasoning. Dump the coated kale in the fryer basket. Set the temperature of your Cuisinart toaster oven to 360 F on Air Fry function and cook for 5 minutes. Shake after 3 minutes. Serve sprinkled with sea salt.

Garlicky Brussels Sprouts

Prep + Cook Time: 30 minutes | Serves: 4

Ingredients

2 tbsp olive oil
1 lb Brussels sprouts, trimmed

2 garlic cloves, chopped
Salt and black pepper to taste

Directions

In a bowl, mix olive oil, garlic, salt, and pepper. Stir in the Brussels sprouts and let rest for 5 minutes. Place the coated sprouts in the fryer basket and fit in the baking tray. Cook in your Cuisinart for 15-18 minutes at 380 F, shaking once. Serve warm.

Cheesy Cabbage Canapes

Prep + Cook Time: 15 minutes | Serves: 4

Ingredients

1 head cabbage, cut in rounds
1 cup mozzarella cheese, grated
½ carrot, cubed

¼ onion, cubed
¼ red bell pepper, chopped
1 tsp fresh basil, chopped

Directions

Preheat Cuisinart on Air Fry function to 360 F. In a bowl, mix onion, carrot, bell pepper, and cheese. Toss to coat everything evenly. Add cabbage rounds to the Air fryer baking pan.

Top with the cheese mixture and cook for 8 minutes. Garnish with basil and serve.

Crispy Bacon with Feta-Butterbean Dip

Prep + Cook Time: 20 minutes | Serves: 2

Ingredients

2 tsp olive oil
1 (14 oz) can butterbeans
1 tbsp chives

½ cup feta, crumbled
Black pepper to taste
8 bacon slices

Directions

Preheat Cuisinart on Air Fry function to 340 F. Arrange the bacon slices on your fryer basket. Sprinkle chives on top and fit in the baking pan. Cook for 6-8 minutes. Blend the beans, olive oil, and black pepper in a blender. Transfer to a bowl and stir in feta cheese until smooth. Serve the bacon with the dip.

Chili Cauliflower Popcorn

Prep + Cook Time: 40 minutes | Serves: 4

Ingredients

1 tbsp olive oil
½ tsp chili powder
½ tsp garlic powder

1 head cauliflower, cut into bite-sized florets
Salt and black pepper to taste
2 tbsp fresh cilantro, chopped

Directions

Preheat Cuisinart on Air Fry function to 380 F. Put the cauliflower, chili powder, garlic powder, salt, pepper, and olive oil in a bowl and toss to coat. Put the frying basket on the baking tray, then spread the cauliflower on the basket in an even layer. Fry for 18-20 minutes. Shake at 10 minutes. Cook until the cauliflower is brown and crunchy. Garnish with cilantro and serve.

Quick Cajun Shrimp

Prep + Cook Time: 20 minutes | Serves: 4

Ingredients

1 tbsp olive oil
1 pound shrimp, deveined
1 tsp Cajun seasoning

Salt and black pepper to taste
¼ tsp smoked paprika
⅛ tsp cayenne pepper

Directions

Preheat Cuisinart on Air Fry function to 390 F. In a bowl, mix the cayenne pepper, smoked paprika, salt, pepper, olive oil, and Cajun seasoning. Add in the shrimp and toss to coat. Transfer the prepared shrimp to the AirFryer basket and fit in the baking tray. Cook for 10-12 minutes, flipping halfway through. Serve immediately.

Bacon-Wrapped Asparagus

Prep + Cook Time: 20 minutes | Serves: 4

Ingredients

1 tbsp olive oil
1 tbsp sesame oil
20 spears asparagus

4 bacon slices
1 tbsp brown sugar
1 garlic clove, minced

Directions

Preheat Cuisinart on Air Fry function to 380 F. In a bowl, mix the oils, brown sugar, and garlic. Separate the asparagus into 4 bunches (5 spears in 1 bunch) and wrap each bunch with a bacon slice. Coat the bunches with the oil mixture. Place them in the fryer basket and fit in the baking tray. Cook for 8 minutes, turning once. Serve warm.

Garam Masala Cashew

Prep + Cook Time: 20 minutes | Serves: 2

Ingredients

2 tbsp mango powder
1 cup cashew nuts
Salt and black pepper to taste

1 tsp coriander powder
½ tsp garam masala powder

Directions

Preheat Cuisinart on Air Fry function to 350 F. In a bowl, mix all powders, salt, and pepper. Add in cashews and toss to coat thoroughly. Place the cashews in your Air Fryer baking pan and cook for 15 minutes, shaking every 5 minutes. Serve.

Simple Cheese Sandwich

Prep + Cook Time: 15 minutes | Serves: 1

Ingredients

2 tbsp butter
2 tbsp Parmesan cheese, shredded
2 scallions, chopped

2 slices bread
¾ cup cheddar cheese

Directions

Preheat Cuisinart on Air Fry function to 360 F. Lay the bread slices on a flat surface. On one slice, spread the exposed side with butter, followed by cheddar and scallions. On the other slice, spread butter and then sprinkle with the Parmesan cheese.

Bring the buttered sides together to form a sandwich. Place it in the cooking basket and cook for 10 minutes. Serve with berry sauce.

Savory Curly Potatoes

Prep + Cook Time: 20 minutes | Serves: 2

Ingredients

1 tbsp extra-virgin olive oil
2 potatoes, spiralized

Salt and black pepper to taste
1 tsp paprika

Directions

Preheat Cuisinart on Air Fry function to 350 F. Place the potatoes in a bowl and coat with oil. Transfer them to the cooking basket and fit in the baking tray. Cook for 15 minutes, shaking once. Sprinkle with salt, pepper, and paprika and serve.

Spiced Parsnip Crisps

Prep + Cook Time: 35 minutes | Serves: 4

Ingredients

2 tbsp olive oil
1 lb parsnips, cut into thin rounds
1 red chili, cut into matchsticks

½ tsp ground cumin
½ tsp ground fennel
Salt and smoked paprika to taste

Directions

Preheat Cuisinart on Air Fry function to 360 F. Place the parsnips into a bowl and drizzle with olive oil. Sprinkle with cumin, fennel, salt, and paprika; toss to coat. Put the frying basket on the baking tray. Spread the parsnips on the basket in an even layer. Air fry for 20-25 minutes, turning once or twice, until golden at the edges. Serve warm sprinkled with chili matchsticks.

Cheese & Chive Scones

Prep + Cook Time: 30 minutes | Serves: 6

Ingredients

¾ oz butter, softened
1 cup flour
1 tsp fresh chives, chopped

1 whole egg
1 tbsp milk
1 cup cheddar cheese, shredded

Directions

Preheat Cuisinart on Air Fry function to 340 F. In a bowl, mix butter, flour, cheddar cheese, chives, milk, and egg to get a sticky dough. Dust a flat surface with flour. Roll the dough into small balls. Place the balls in the baking pan and cook for 20 minutes. Serve and enjoy!

Homemade Cheddar Biscuits

Prep + Cook Time: 40 minutes | Serves: 6

Ingredients

½ cup + 1 tbsp butter
1 tbsp sugar
3 cups flour

1 ⅓ cups buttermilk
½ cup cheddar cheese, grated

Directions

Preheat Cuisinart on Bake function to 380 F. Lay parchment paper on a baking plate. In a bowl, mix sugar, flour, ½ cup of butter, half of the cheddar cheese, and buttermilk to form a batter.

Make 8 balls from the batter and roll in flour. Place the balls in your Air Fryer baking tray and flatten into biscuit shapes. Sprinkle the remaining cheddar cheese and remaining butter on top. Cook for 30 minutes, tossing every 10 minutes. Serve chilled.

Air Fried Mac & Cheese

Prep + Cook Time: 15 minutes | Serves: 1

Ingredients

1 cup cooked macaroni
1 cup grated cheddar cheese
½ cup warm milk

1 tbsp Parmesan cheese
Salt and black pepper to taste

Directions

Preheat Cuisinart on Air Fry function to 350 F. Add the macaroni to Air Fryer baking pan. Stir in the cheddar cheese and milk. Season with salt and pepper. Place the dish in the toaster oven and cook for 10 minutes. Sprinkle with Parmesan cheese and serve.

Easy Parsnip Fries

Prep + Cook Time: 20 minutes | Serves: 3

Ingredients

¼ cup olive oil

4 parsnips, sliced

¼ cup flour

A pinch of salt

Directions

Preheat Cuisinart on Air Fry to 390 F. In a bowl, add the flour, olive oil, ¼ cup of water, salt, and parsnips; mix to coat. Line the fries on the greased fryer basket and cook for 15 minutes.

Crispy Eggplant Fries

Prep + Cook Time: 20 minutes | Serves: 2

Ingredients

1 tsp olive oil

1 eggplant, sliced

1 tsp soy sauce

Salt to taste

Directions

Preheat Cuisinart on Air Fry function to 400 F. Coat the eggplant with olive oil, soy sauce, and salt. Place it in the cooking basket and fit in the baking tray. Cook for 8 minutes. Serve warm.

Homemade Prosciutto Wrapped Cheese Sticks

Prep + Cook Time: 20 minutes | Serves: 6

Ingredients

1 lb cheddar cheese

12 prosciutto slices

Directions

Preheat Cuisinart on Air Fry function to 390 F. Cut the cheese into 6 equal sticks. Wrap each piece with 2 prosciutto slices. Place them in the basket and cook for 10 minutes, turning once.

Caramelized Root Vegetable Medley

Prep + Cook Time: 30 minutes | Serves: 4

Ingredients

2 tbsp rapeseed oil

3 tsp brown sugar

1 beet, cut into chunks

1 small sweet potato, cut into chunks

2 carrots, cut into chunks

2 parsnips, cut into chunks

¼ tsp ground cinnamon

Salt to taste

Directions

Preheat Cuisinart on Air Fry function to 360 F. In a bowl, mix the root vegetables, brown sugar, oil, cinnamon, and salt; toss to coat. Spread on the frying basket and fry for 20 minutes. Shake the basket at 10 minutes. The finished veggies should be soft and lightly caramelized.

Pineapple & Mozzarella Tortilla Pizzas

Prep + Cook Time: 20 minutes | Serves: 2

Ingredients

2 tortillas
4 ham slices
¼ cup mozzarella cheese, grated

2 thin pineapple slices
2 tbsp tomato sauce
½ tsp dried parsley

Directions

Preheat Cuisinart on Air Fry function to 330 F. Spread the tomato sauce onto the tortillas. Arrange 2 ham slices on each tortilla. Top the ham with the pineapple and sprinkle with mozzarella and parsley. Cook for 10 minutes until golden brown on top. Serve and enjoy!

Tasty Carrot Chips

Prep + Cook Time: 20 minutes | Serves: 2

Ingredients

3 large carrots, sliced heightwise

Salt to taste

Directions

Salt the carrot strips and place them in the fryer basket. Cook in the Cuisinart at 350 F for 10 minutes on Air Fry function, stirring once halfway through. Serve warm.

Russian-Style Eggplant Caviar

Prep + Cook Time: 25 minutes | Serves: 3

Ingredients

3 tbsp olive oil
3 medium eggplants
½ red onion, chopped

2 tbsp balsamic vinegar
Salt to taste

Directions

Arrange the eggplants on the frying basket and cook them in your Cuisinart for 15 minutes at 380 F on Bake function. Let cool. Peel and chop the cooled eggplants. Process the onion and eggplant in a blender until smooth. Add in the vinegar, olive oil, and salt, then blend again.

POULTRY RECIPES

Chicken Breasts with Tomato-Cheese Topping

Prep + Cook Time: 20 minutes | Serves: 2

Ingredients

2 chicken breasts, sliced
2 eggs, beaten
1 cup breadcrumbs
Salt and black pepper to taste

2 tbsp tomato sauce
2 tbsp Romano cheese, grated
2 slices mozzarella cheese

Directions

Preheat Cuisinart on Air Fry function to 400 F. Season the breasts with salt and pepper. Dip the breasts into the eggs, then into the crumbs, and arrange them on a greased baking tray. Cook for 5 minutes. Turn and top with tomato sauce, Romano and mozzarella cheeses. Cook for 5 more minutes until the cheese is melted. Serve warm.

Sticky Dijon Chicken Thighs

Prep + Cook Time: 25 minutes | Serves: 4

Ingredients

4 chicken thighs, skin-on
2 tbsp honey
1 tbsp Dijon mustard

½ tbsp garlic powder
Salt and black pepper to taste

Directions

In a bowl, mix honey, mustard, garlic, salt, and black pepper. Coat the thighs with the mixture and arrange them on the greased basket. Fit in the baking tray and cook in your Cuisinart for 18-20 minutes at 400 F on Air Fry function, turning halfway through. Serve warm.

Chicken Strips with Hot Aioli Sauce

Prep + Cook Time: 25 minutes | Serves: 4

Ingredients

2 tbsp olive oil
1 lb chicken breasts, cut into strips
1 cup breadcrumbs
Salt and black pepper to taste

½ tbsp garlic powder
½ cup mayonnaise
1 tbsp lemon juice
½ tbsp ground chili

Directions

Mix breadcrumbs, salt, pepper, and garlic and spread onto a plate. Brush the chicken with olive oil, then roll it up in the breadcrumb mixture. Arrange on the oiled frying basket and fit in the baking tray; cook for 14-16 minutes in your Cuisinart at 360 F on Air Fry function, turning once.

To prepare the aioli: mix well mayonnaise with lemon juice, salt, pepper, and chili. Serve the chicken with hot aioli.

Parmesan Chicken Fingers with Plum Sauce

Prep + Cook Time: 20 minutes | Serves: 2

Ingredients

2 chicken breasts, cut into strips
2 tbsp Parmesan cheese, grated
¼ tbsp fresh chives, chopped
⅓ cup breadcrumbs
1 egg white

2 tbsp plum sauce
½ tbsp fresh thyme, chopped
½ tbsp black pepper
1 tbsp water

Directions

Preheat Cuisinart on Air Fry function to 360 F. Mix the chives, Parmesan cheese, thyme, pepper, and breadcrumbs. In another bowl, whisk the egg white with the water. Dip the chicken strips into the egg mixture and then in the breadcrumb mixture. Place the strips in the greased basket and fit in the baking tray. Cook for 10 minutes, flipping once. Serve with plum sauce.

Mango Marinated Chicken Breasts

Prep + Cook Time: 25 minutes + marinating time| Serves: 2

Ingredients

2 tbsp olive oil
2 chicken breasts, cubed
1 large mango, cubed
1 red pepper, chopped

2 tbsp balsamic vinegar
2 garlic cloves, minced
1 tbsp fresh parsley, chopped
Salt to taste

Directions

In a bowl, mix mango, garlic, red pepper, olive oil, salt, and balsamic vinegar. Add the mixture to a blender and pulse until smooth. Transfer to a bowl and add in the chicken cubes. Toss to coat and place in the fridge for 30 minutes.

Preheat Cuisinart on Air Fry function to 360 F. Remove the chicken from the fridge and place cubes in the greased basket. Fit in the baking tray and cook in the air fryer oven for 14-16 minutes, shaking once. Garnish with parsley and serve immediately.

Herby Chicken with Lime

Prep + Cook Time: 75 minutes + chilling time| Serves: 4

Ingredients

2 tbsp olive oil
1 (3 ½-lb) whole chicken
Salt and black pepper to taste
½ tbsp chili powder
½ tbsp garlic powder

1 tbsp oregano
½ tbsp cilantro powder
½ tbsp cumin powder
1 tbsp paprika
1 lime, juiced

Directions

In a bowl, put oregano, garlic powder, chili powder, cilantro, paprika, cumin, pepper, salt, and olive oil. Mix well and rub the mixture onto the chicken. Refrigerate for 20 minutes.

Preheat Cuisinart on Air Fry function to 350 F. Remove the chicken from the refrigerator; place in the greased basket and fit in the baking tray; cook for 45 minutes. Use a skewer to poke the chicken to ensure that it is clear of juices. If not, cook further for 5 to 10 minutes; let it rest for 10 minutes. Drizzle lime juice all over and serve with a green salad.

Fried Chicken Tenderloins

Prep + Cook Time: 25 minutes | Serves: 4

Ingredients

2 tbsp butter, melted
8 chicken tenderloins

2 oz breadcrumbs
1 large egg, whisked

Directions

Preheat Cuisinart on Air Fry function to 380 F. Dip the chicken in the egg, then in the crumbs, and drizzle with melted butter. Place in the basket and fit in the baking tray. Cook for 14-16 minutes, flipping once, until crispy. Set on Broil function for crispier taste. Serve.

Ham & Cheese Stuffed Chicken Breasts

Prep + Cook Time: 40 minutes | Serves: 4

Ingredients

4 tbsp butter
4 skinless and boneless chicken breasts
4 ham slices
4 Swiss cheese slices
3 tbsp all-purpose flour

1 tbsp paprika
1 tbsp chicken bouillon granules
½ cup dry white wine
1 cup heavy whipping cream

Directions

Preheat Cuisinart on Air Fry function to 380 F. Pound the chicken breasts and top each with a slice of ham and a slice of Swiss cheese. Fold the edges of the chicken over the filling and secure the borders with toothpicks. In a medium bowl, combine the paprika and flour; coat the chicken rolls with the mixture. Fry the chicken in your Cuisinart for 20 minutes, turning once.

In a large skillet over low heat, melt the butter and add the heavy cream, bouillon granules, and wine; bring to a boil. Add in the chicken and let simmer for around 5-10 minutes. Serve.

Chicken Wrapped in Turkey Bacon

Prep + Cook Time: 25 minutes | Serves: 2

Ingredients

1 tbsp butter, melted
2 chicken breast fillets
½ tsp Italian seasoning
6 turkey bacon slices

Salt and black pepper to taste
1 tbsp fresh parsley, chopped
Juice from ½ lemon

Directions

Preheat Cuisinart on Bake function to 390 F. Season the chicken with Italian seasoning, salt, and black pepper. Wrap 3 bacon slices around fillets. Place the wrapped chicken in the AirFryer basket and fit in the baking tray. Brush with melted butter.

Cook for 14-16 minutes, turning over a couple of times. Remove the chicken to a serving platter and top with parsley and lemon juice. Serve with steamed greens if desired.

Cayenne Chicken Drumsticks with Peppers

Prep + Cook Time: 30 minutes | Serves: 4

Ingredients

8 chicken drumsticks
1 tsp oregano
1 tsp thyme
½ cup cornflakes

2 eggs
½ tsp cayenne powder
1 red bell pepper, sliced
Salt and black pepper to taste

Directions

Preheat Cuisinart on Air Fry function to 350 F. Coat the drumsticks with oregano, thyme, cayenne powder, salt, and pepper. Dip drumsticks into the eggs first and then into the cornflakes. Arrange on the greased AirFryer basket and fit in the baking tray. Cook for 10 minutes. Sprinkle the bell pepper with salt and pepper and place them around the chicken. Continue cooking for 10 minutes until golden brown. Serve warm.

Chicken Carnitas

Prep + Cook Time: 30 minutes | Serves: 4

Ingredients

2 tbsp olive oil
1 pound chicken breasts, sliced
1 red bell pepper, thinly sliced
1 green bell pepper, thinly sliced
1 small red onion, thinly sliced
1 ½ tsp fajita seasoning
½ tsp garlic powder
¼ tsp onion powder

¼ tsp chili powder
1 tsp chipotle sauce
8 tortillas
1 ancho chili pepper, finely chopped
½ cup guacamole
½ cup sour cream
2 tbsp fresh cilantro, chopped

Directions

Preheat Cuisinart on Air Fry function to 380 F. In a mixing bowl, combine the red onion, olive oil, fajita seasoning, garlic powder, onion powder, chili powder, and chipotle sauce until well mixed. Add the chicken and bell peppers and toss until everything is well coated.

Distribute the chicken and veggies on the baking sheet. Cook for 15 minutes, stirring halfway through the cooking time until the chicken is browned and the vegetables are lightly wilted. Divide the chicken and veggies between the tortilla, top with sour cream, guacamole, ancho chili pepper, and cilantro. Roll up and serve immediately.

Chicken Parmigiana

Prep + Cook Time: 35 minutes | Serves: 2

Ingredients

½ cup flour
2 fresh eggs
4 tbsp Parmesan cheese, grated
½ cup panko breadcrumbs
½ tsp garlic powder

2 chicken breasts, halved widthwise
1 cup passata (tomato sauce)
1 tsp dried rosemary
1 tbsp fresh basil leaves, chiffonade
¾ cup provolone cheese, shredded

Directions

Preheat Cuisinart on Air Fry function to 395 F. Beat the eggs in a bowl. Combine the Parmesan cheese and breadcrumbs in a separate bowl. Mix the flour, garlic powder, and rosemary on a plate. Roll the chicken in the flour, then in the eggs, and finally, coat in the crumbs mixture.

Lay the chicken in the greased baking pan and spritz both sides with cooking spray. Cook for about 8 minutes, flip, and cook for an additional 7 minutes. Then, remove the pan and pour the passata in equal amounts over the chicken pieces. Top with the provolone cheese, return to the oven; cook for 5 minutes, or until the cheese is bubbling and golden. Sprinkle with basil.

Korean-Style Chicken Wings

Prep + Cook Time: 30 minutes | Serves: 4

Ingredients

2 tbsp canola oil
1 pound chicken wings
1 cup flour
1 cup breadcrumbs
2 eggs, beaten
Salt and black pepper to taste

2 tbsp sesame seeds
2 tbsp Gochujang (Korean red pepper paste)
1 tbsp apple cider vinegar
2 tbsp honey
1 tbsp soy sauce

Directions

Preheat Cuisinart on Air Fry function to 360 F. Separate the chicken wings into winglets and drumettes. Sprinkle the chicken pieces with salt and pepper. Coat them with flour, followed by eggs and breadcrumbs. Place them in the basket and fit in the baking tray. Drizzle with canola oil and cook for 14-16 minutes, flipping halfway through.

Mix the Gochujang, apple cider vinegar, soy sauce, honey, and ¼ cup of water in a saucepan and bring to a boil over medium heat. Simmer until the sauce thickens, about 4 minutes. Pour the sauce over the chicken pieces. Garnish with sesame seeds and serve.

Tandoori-Spiced Chicken Thighs

Prep + Cook Time: 40 minutes + marinating time | Serves: 4

Ingredients

4 skinless, boneless chicken thighs
1 cup Greek yogurt
¼ sweet onion, finely chopped
2 tsp Tandoori masala
1 garlic clove, minced
1-inch fresh ginger piece, grated
½ tsp ground cumin

½ tsp ground coriander
¼ tsp sea salt
⅛ tsp cayenne powder
1 lemon, cut into wedges
2 tbsp cilantro, chopped
½ red chili, finely sliced

Directions

Combine yogurt, onion, tandoori masala, garlic, ginger, cumin, coriander, salt, and cayenne; mix well. Add in the chicken and toss to coat. Cover with foil and put in the fridge for 2 hours.

Preheat Cuisinart on Air Fry function to 370 degrees. Remove the chicken thighs, shake the extra marinade off, and lay them in the greased frying basket. Discard the rest of the marinade. Fit the basket in the baking tray and coat the chicken with cooking spray. Cook for 15 minutes, turn, then cook for another 12-15 minutes or until the internal temperature is 160 F. Garnish the chicken with cilantro, chopped chili, and lemon wedges and serve.

Chinese Sticky Chicken Thighs

Prep + Cook Time: 30 minutes + chilling time | Serves: 2

Ingredients

1 tbsp sesame oil
½ tsp Chinese five-spice powder
2 tbsp soy sauce
1 tbsp brown sugar
1 tbsp balsamic vinegar
1 tbsp sweet chili sauce

1 lime, juiced
1 garlic clove, minced
1 tsp ginger puree
2 chicken thighs
1 scallion, thinly sliced
2 tsp sesame seeds

Directions

Stir five-spice powder, soy sauce, sesame oil, brown sugar, balsamic vinegar, chili sauce, lime juice, garlic, and ginger in a bowl. Add in the chicken; toss to coat. Put in the fridge for 1 hour.

Preheat Cuisinart on Air Fry function to 390 F. Remove the chicken from the fridge. Put the frying basket on the baking tray and coat it with cooking spray. Lay the thighs on the basket and cook for 18-22 minutes. When ready, the thighs should be golden and caramelized. Top with scallion and sesame seeds and serve.

Caribbean-Inspired Chicken Skewers

Prep + Cook Time: 30 minutes | Serves: 2

Ingredients

2 chicken breasts, cubed
½ green bell pepper, sliced
½ red bell pepper, sliced

1 shallot, cut into wedges
1 can drain pineapple chunks
½ cup sriracha sauce

Directions

Preheat Cuisinart on Bake function to 370 F. Thread the bell peppers, chicken cubes, shallot, and pineapple chunks on the skewers. Brush with sriracha sauce and cook in your Cuisinart for 20 minutes, turning once, until slightly crispy. Serve immediately.

Worcestershire Chicken Breasts

Prep + Cook Time: 40 minutes | Serves: 4

Ingredients

2 tbsp olive oil
Salt and black pepper to taste
4 chicken breasts, sliced
¼ cup Worcestershire sauce

¼ tsp onion powder
¼ tsp garlic powder
¼ tsp yellow mustard

Directions

In a bowl, whisk the olive oil, onion powder, garlic powder, mustard, salt, and pepper. Add in the chicken and let sit for 10 minutes. Preheat Cuisinart on Air Fry function to 360 F. Arrange the chicken slices on a greased baking tray. Pour the Worcestershire sauce over them and cook for 18-22 minutes, shaking once, until done. Serve immediately.

Buffalo Chicken Wing Drumettes

Prep + Cook Time: 30 minutes + chilling time | Serves: 4

Ingredients

2 pounds chicken wing drumettes
¼ cup ketchup
¼ cup BBQ sauce
1 tbsp Tabasco sauce

2 scallions, sliced diagonally
¼ tsp cayenne pepper
¼ tsp chili powder

Directions

In a large bowl, mix well ketchup, barbecue sauce, tabasco sauce, cayenne pepper, and chili powder. Add in the chicken wing drumettes and toss until well coated. Cover with foil and marinate in the refrigerator for 2 hours.

Preheat Cuisinart on Air Fry function to 390 F. Place the chicken wing drumettes on a greased baking tray and cook for 18-20 minutes. When cooking is complete, the chicken wings should be cooked, and the marinade should be sticky. Serve topped with scallions, and enjoy!

Homemade Rotisserie Chicken

Prep + Cook Time: 90 minutes | Serves: 4

Ingredients

¼ cup butter, melted
1 (3.5-pound) whole chicken
1 tsp paprika
1 tsp cayenne pepper

1 tsp dried rosemary
1 tsp dried thyme
Salt and black pepper to taste

Directions

Preheat your Cuisinart oven to 380 F on Bake function. In a small bowl, combine the paprika, cayenne pepper, rosemary, thyme, salt, pepper, and butter and stir well. Rub the chicken with the spice mixture and put it on the aluminum foil-lined baking tray.

Cook for 60-70 minutes or until the skin is slightly-charred and a meat thermometer inserted in the thickest part of the thigh registers 165 F . Allow the chicken to cool for 10 minutes before carving. Serve and enjoy!

Southern Fried Chicken

Prep + Cook Time: 30 minutes + marinating time | Serves: 4

Ingredients

1 tbsp sriracha sauce
1 tsp turmeric
1 ½ lb chicken drumsticks
1 cup buttermilk
1 cup flour
1 tbsp smoked paprika
¾ tsp ground celery seeds

¾ tsp mustard powder
½ tsp garlic powder
Salt and black pepper to taste
½ tsp dried thyme
¼ tsp dried oregano
½ cup breadcrumbs
4 large eggs

Directions

In a bowl, combine the sriracha sauce and buttermilk and add the chicken. Toss to coat, cover with a lid and marinate in the fridge for at least 4 hours.

Preheat Cuisinart on Air Fry function to 370 degrees. Whisk the eggs until frothy in a bowl. Combine the flour, turmeric, paprika, ground celery seeds, mustard powder, garlic powder, pepper, salt, thyme, and oregano in another bowl. Spread the breadcrumbs onto a large plate.

Coat the fryer basket with cooking spray and fit it in the baking tray. Roll the chicken in the flour mixture, then dip in the eggs, then coat in the crumbs. Place on the basket and spritz all sides with cooking spray. Cook for 10 minutes, flip, and cook for another 10 minutes. When cooking is complete, the chicken should be golden and crunchy. Serve hot.

Hawaiian-Style Chicken Bites

Prep + Cook Time: 25 minutes + chilling time | Serves: 4

Ingredients

1 lb chicken breasts, cubed
1 tbsp hot chili sauce
1 tbsp brown sugar
½ cup pineapple juice
1 lime, juiced

¼ cup soy sauce
2 garlic cloves, minced
½ tbsp ginger, minced
1 tsp sherry

Directions

Place the chicken in a bowl. Mix the hot chili sauce, brown sugar, pineapple juice, lime juice, soy sauce, garlic, ginger, and sherry in another bowl and stir until the sugar dissolves. Pour the marinade over the chicken, cover with foil, and place in the refrigerator for 2 hours.

Preheat your Cuisinart oven on Air Fry function to 360 F. Remove the chicken from the marinade, pat dry, and place it in the greased basket. Spritz the chicken with cooking spray and cook for 14-16 minutes, shaking once, until cooked through. Serve warm.

Cheesy Chicken Enchiladas

Prep + Cook Time: 30 minutes | Serves: 4

Ingredients

2 tbsp olive oil
3 cups cooked chicken, shredded
1 onion, sliced
2 garlic cloves, minced
1 cup canned black beans
1 cup red roasted peppers, chopped

Salt and black pepper to taste
1 tsp California chili powder
1 cup Colby cheese, grated
1 cup salsa
12 flour tortillas
1 cup enchilada sauce

Directions

Preheat Cuisinart on Bake function to 380 F. Warm the olive oil in a saucepan over medium heat and stir-fry the onion and garlic for 3 minutes. Stir in chili powder, salt, and pepper for 1 minute. Pour in half of the salsa, peppers, black beans, and chicken and stir well; set aside.

In a bowl, mix the remaining salsa and enchilada sauce. Divide the chicken mixture between the tortillas. Roll up the tortillas and transfer them to the lightly greased cooking basket, seam-side down. Spoon over the enchilada mixture and sprinkle with the Colby cheese. Cook for 10-14 minutes, turning them over halfway through until the cheese is golden and bubbling.

Chicken Schnitzel Cordon Bleu

Prep + Cook Time: 35 minutes | Serves: 4

Ingredients

4 chicken breasts, halved lengthwise
4 Swiss cheese slices
4 ham slices
1 cup flour
1 tsp garlic powder

Salt and black pepper to taste
2 fresh eggs
1 cup panko breadcrumbs
½ cup Parmesan cheese

Directions

Preheat your Cuisinart oven to 400 F on Air Fry function. Cover the chicken pieces with plastic wrap and pound them to ½-inch thickness using a meat mallet. Put a slice of cheese and ham in the middle of each breast. "Close the books" or fold the sides over the cheese and ham. Roll the breasts up from the unfolded side to seal and secure with toothpicks.

Prepare 3 mixing dishes. In the first one, pour the flour with garlic powder. In another mixing dish, whisk the eggs. In the third dish, combine the Parmesan cheese, panko breadcrumbs, salt, and pepper. Roll the chicken in the flour, then place in the eggs, then coat well in the crumbs.

Place the schnitzels in the basket and fit in the baking tray. Spritz the chicken with cooking spray. Fry for about 18-22 minutes, flipping halfway through the cooking time. Serve and enjoy!

Curried Chicken Wings

Prep + Cook Time: 20 minutes + chilling time| Serves: 2

Ingredients

8 chicken wings
1 tbsp water
2 tbsp potato starch

2 tbsp hot curry paste
½ tbsp baking powder

Directions

Combine hot curry paste and water in a small bowl. Add in the wings and toss to coat. Cover the bowl with plastic wrap and refrigerate for 30 minutes.

Preheat Cuisinart on Air Fry function to 370 degrees. In a bowl, mix baking powder with potato starch. Remove the wings from the fridge and dip them in the starch mixture. Place on a lined baking dish and cook in your Cuisinart for 7 minutes. Flip over and cook for 5 minutes. Serve.

Sticky Chinese-Style Chicken Wings

Prep + Cook Time: 30 minutes | Serves: 4

Ingredients

1 lb chicken wings
1 tbsp cilantro leaves, chopped
Salt and black pepper to taste
1 tbsp roasted peanuts, chopped
½ tbsp apple cider vinegar

1 garlic clove, minced
½ tbsp chili sauce
1-inch ginger piece, minced
1 ½ tbsp soy sauce
1 tbsp honey

Directions

In a bowl, mix ginger, garlic, chili sauce, honey, soy sauce, cilantro, salt, pepper, and vinegar. Add in the chicken and toss to coat. Place the chicken in the greased basket and fit in the baking tray. Cook in your Cuisinart for 20 minutes at 360 F on Air Fry. Serve sprinkled with peanuts.

Chicken with Avocado & Radish Bowl

Prep + Cook Time: 25 minutes | Serves: 2

Ingredients

1 tbsp sesame oil
½ chicken tenderloins
¼ cup Parmesan cheese, grated
¼ cup flour
¼ tsp garlic powder
¼ tsp chili powder

½ tbsp lime juice
1 avocado, sliced
4 radishes, sliced
1 tbsp chopped parsley
Salt and black pepper to taste

Directions

Preheat Cuisinart on Air Fry function to 300 F. In a bowl, combine the Parmesan cheese, flour, garlic powder, chili powder, salt, and pepper. Coat the chicken tenderloins with the mixture.

Spritz them with cooking spray and transfer to the fryer basket. Cook for 14-16 minutes, shaking once. Combine the avocado, radishes, lime juice, sesame oil, parsley, and salt in a salad bowl and serve with the chicken tenderloins. Enjoy!

Beer-Battered Chicken Wings with Hot Sauce

Prep + Cook Time: 35 minutes | Serves: 4

Ingredients

1 tbsp olive oil
2 pounds chicken wings
Salt and black pepper to taste
½ cup flour

½ cup cornstarch
¼ tsp garlic powder
½ cup light beer
¼ cup hot sauce

Directions

Preheat your Cuisinart oven to 400 F on Air Fry function. Using a sharp knife, cut off the chicken wings' tips and divide them into flats and drumettes. Season with salt and pepper.

In a large bowl, combine the flour, cornstarch, garlic powder, and beer and mix well. Coat the chicken pieces with the batter. Put the chicken wings into the greased basket and fit in the baking tray. Cook in the upper position for 20-25 minutes until golden and crispy. In a bowl, whisk the hot sauce and olive oil. Add in the cooked wings and toss to coat. Serve.

Harissa Chicken Wings

Prep + Cook Time: 30 minutes | Serves: 4

Ingredients

2 pounds chicken wings
¾ cup flour
1 tsp garlic powder

1 tsp harissa spice blend
Salt and black pepper to taste
¼ tsp shallot powder

Directions

Preheat Cuisinart on Air Fry function to 390 F. Fit the fryer basket in the baking tray and coat with cooking spray. Combine the flour, garlic powder, harissa, salt, pepper, and shallot powder in a bowl. Toss the chicken wings in the bowl and shake to coat.

Place them in the basket, spritzing both sides with cooking spray. Cook for 10 minutes, flip, then cook for 10 more minutes. Serve hot.

Asian Chicken Wings

Prep + Cook Time: 30 minutes | Serves: 2

Ingredients

1 lb chicken wings
2 tbsp sweet chili sauce
¼ tsp cayenne pepper
1 garlic clove, minced

¼ tsp ginger powder
½ tbsp lime juice
½ tbsp honey
Salt and black pepper to taste

Directions

Preheat Cuisinart on Air Fry function to 350 F. Mix the sweet chili sauce, cayenne pepper, garlic, ginger powder, lime juice, honey, salt, and pepper in a bowl. Pour the mixture over the chicken wings and toss to coat. Put the chicken wings in the basket and fit in the baking tray; cook for 25 minutes. Shake every 5 minutes. Serve.

Mom's Tarragon Chicken Breast Packets

Prep + Cook Time: 20 minutes | Serves: 2

Ingredients

1 tbsp butter
2 chicken breasts

Salt and black pepper to taste
¼ tsp dried tarragon

Directions

Preheat Cuisinart on Bake function to 380 F. Place each chicken breast on a foil wrap. Top with tarragon and butter and season with salt and pepper. Wrap the foil around the chicken breasts in a loose way to create a flow of air. Cook the in your Cuisinart oven for 15 minutes. Remove and carefully unwrap. Slice and serve. Enjoy!

Marinara Chicken Breasts

Prep + Cook Time: 20 minutes | Serves: 2

Ingredients

2 chicken breasts, ½ inch thick
1 egg, beaten
½ cup breadcrumbs

2 tbsp marinara sauce
2 tbsp Grana Padano cheese, grated
2 slices mozzarella cheese

Directions

Dip the breasts into the egg, then into the crumbs, and arrange on the Air fryer baking sheet. Cook for 6-8 minutes at 400 F on Air Fry function. Turn over and drizzle with marinara sauce, Grana Padano and mozzarella cheeses. Cook for 5 more minutes. Serve.

Parmesan Chicken Cutlets

Prep + Cook Time: 30 minutes | Serves: 4

Ingredients

¼ cup Parmesan cheese, grated

4 chicken cutlets

⅛ tbsp paprika

2 tbsp panko breadcrumbs

½ tbsp garlic powder

2 large eggs, beaten

Directions

In a bowl, mix Parmesan cheese, breadcrumbs, garlic powder, and paprika. Add eggs to another bowl. Dip the chicken in eggs, dredge them in the cheese mixture and place them in the basket; fit in the baking tray. Cook for 20-25 minutes on Air Fry function at 400 F.

Chicken with Peppercorns & Lemon

Prep + Cook Time: 20 minutes | Serves: 1

Ingredients

1 chicken breast

2 lemon, juiced and rind reserved

½ tsp poultry seasoning

1 tsp garlic puree

A tsp peppercorns

Salt to taste

Directions

Place a silver foil sheet on a flat surface. Add all seasonings alongside the lemon rind. Lay the chicken breast onto a chopping board and trim any fat. Rub the chicken with the seasoning and salt on both sides. Place on the silver foil sheet. Seal tightly and flatten with a rolling pin.

Place the breast in the basket and fit in the baking tray; cook for 15 minutes at 350 F on Air Fry function. Serve hot.

Easy Peasy Mayo Cheesy Chicken

Prep + Cook Time: 25 minutes | Serves: 4

Ingredients

4 chicken breasts, cubed

1 tbsp garlic powder

1 cup mayonnaise

Salt to taste

½ cup soft cheese

2 tbsp chopped basil

Directions

Preheat your Cuisinart oven to 400 F on Bake function. In a bowl, mix the cheese, mayonnaise, garlic powder, and salt. Cover your chicken with the mixture. Place the chicken in the basket and fit in the baking tray; cook for 16-18 minutes. Serve garnished with chopped fresh basil.

Cheesy Chicken Escallops

Prep + Cook Time: 20 minutes | Serves: 4

Ingredients

4 skinless chicken breasts
¼ cup panko breadcrumbs
2 tbsp Parmesan cheese, grated

6 sage leaves, chopped
¼ cup seasoned flour
2 eggs, beaten

Directions

Place the chicken breasts between a cling film, beat well using a rolling pin until a ½ inch thickness is achieved. In a bowl, add Parmesan cheese, sage, and breadcrumbs. Dredge the chicken into the seasoned flour and then into the eggs. Finally, coat in the breadcrumbs.

Spray the chicken breasts with cooking spray and cook in your Cuisinart oven for 14-16 minutes at 350 F on Air Fry function. Serve and enjoy!

Basil Mozzarella Chicken

Prep + Cook Time: 35 minutes | Serves: 4

Ingredients

1 tbsp butter
4 chicken breasts, cubed
4 basil leaves

¼ cup balsamic vinegar
4 tomato slices
4 mozzarella cheese slices

Directions

Preheat Cuisinart on Bake function to 400 F. Heat butter and balsamic vinegar in a pan over medium heat. Place the chicken in a baking pan and pour over the butter/balsamic mixture. Bake for 20 minutes. Cover with the cheese slices and Bake for another 4-5 minutes until the cheese melts. Top with basil and tomato slices and serve.

Garlic-Lemon Stuffed Chicken

Prep + Cook Time: 75 minutes | Serves: 4

Ingredients

4 tbsp olive oil
1 (3 ½ pounds) whole chicken
Salt and black pepper to taste

1 lemon, cut into quarters
5 garlic cloves, peeled
1 tbsp dried mixed herbs

Directions

Preheat Cuisinart on Air Fry function to 360 F. Brush the chicken with olive oil and season with salt and black pepper. Stuff the chicken cavity with lemon, herbs, and garlic cloves.

Place the chicken breast-side down onto the frying basket. Tuck the legs and wings tips under. Fit in the baking tray and cook for 45-60 minutes, flipping halfway through the cooking time. Let rest for 5-6 minutes, then carve, and serve.

Coconut Fried Chicken

Prep + Cook Time: 20 minutes | Serves: 4

Ingredients

2 large eggs, beaten

2 tbsp garlic powder

Salt and black pepper to taste

¾ cup breadcrumbs

¾ cup shredded coconut

1 pound chicken tenders

Directions

Preheat your Cuisinart on Air Fry function to 400 F. Spritz the frying basket with cooking spray and fit it in a baking tray. In a deep dish, whisk the garlic powder, eggs, pepper, and salt. In another bowl, mix the breadcrumbs and coconut.

Dip your chicken tenders in egg mixture, then in the coconut mix; shake off any excess. Place the prepared chicken tenders in the greased basket and fit in the baking tray; cook for 12-14 minutes until golden brown. Serve.

Thai Turkey Meatballs

Prep + Cook Time: 30 minutes | Serves: 4

Ingredients

1 tsp Thai seasoning blend

1 ¼ pounds ground turkey

½ cup breadcrumbs

1 large egg

1 spring onion, finely chopped

¼ cup coconut milk

¼ cup unsweetened coconut, shredded

1 tbsp fish sauce

1 garlic clove, minced

1-inch fresh ginger piece, grated

2 tbsp cilantro, chopped

1 lime, cut into wedges

Directions

Preheat Cuisinart on Bake function to 350 F. Toss the Thai seasoning, ground turkey, breadcrumbs, egg, spring onion, coconut milk, coconut, fish sauce, garlic, and ginger into a bowl and mix well. Make 1-inch balls out of the turkey mix. Lay them on the baking sheet in a single layer.

Cook for 10 minutes, turn the balls, and cook for another 10 minutes. When cooking is complete, the meatballs should be browned. Serve garnished with cilantro and lime wedges.

Chicken Wings with Yogurt Sauce

Prep + Cook Time: 20 minutes | Serves: 4

Ingredients

2 pounds chicken wings
Salt and black pepper to taste
1 ½ tsp ground cumin
1 tbsp cilantro, chopped

1 garlic clove, minced
1 cup yogurt
½ tbsp lemon juice
½ tbsp ginger, minced

Directions

Preheat Cuisinart on Air Fry to 360 F. Season the chicken wings with cumin, salt, and pepper, place them in the basket, and fit in the baking tray. Cook for 15 minutes, shaking once. In a bowl, mix the remaining ingredients. Serve the chicken with the yogurt sauce and enjoy!

Za'atar Chicken Tenders

Prep + Cook Time: 45 minutes | Serves: 4

Ingredients

1 tbsp olive oil
½ lime, juiced
½ tsp Za'atar seasoning
½ chili powder

1 garlic clove, minced
1 pound chicken breasts
Salt and black pepper to taste

Directions

Preheat your Cuisinart to 360 F on Bake function. Combine the lime juice, Za'atar seasoning, chili powder, and garlic in a bowl. Rub salt and pepper all over the chicken breasts.

Warm the olive oil in a skillet over medium heat and sear the chicken on all sides for 5-6 minutes or until slightly browned. Place them on the frying basket and fit in the baking tray.

Use a cooking brush to rub the Za'atar mixture onto the breasts. Cook for 10 minutes, brush more mixture over the chicken, then cook for another 10 minutes until the meat reaches an internal temperature of 145 F. Let cool for around 10 minutes, then serve warm.

Whole Chicken with BBQ Sauce

Prep + Cook Time: 40 minutes | Serves: 4

Ingredients

1 (3.5-pound) whole chicken, cut into pieces
Salt to taste
1 tsp smoked paprika

1 tsp garlic powder
1 cup BBQ sauce

Directions

Coat the chicken with salt, paprika, and garlic. Place the chicken pieces skin-side down in the greased baking tray. Cook in the Cuisinart oven for around 20-25 minutes at 400 F on Bake function until slightly golden. Remove to a plate and brush with barbecue sauce. Return the chicken to the oven skin-side up and cook for 5 minutes at 340 F. Serve with more BBQ sauce.

Thyme Turkey Nuggets

Prep + Cook Time: 25 minutes | Serves: 2

Ingredients

½ lb turkey breast, cut into bite-sized pieces
1 egg, beaten

1 cup breadcrumbs
Salt and dried thyme to taste

Directions

Preheat Cuisinart on Air Fry function to 350 F. Coat the turkey with thyme and salt. Roll first in the breadcrumbs, then dip into the beaten egg. Lastly, roll in the breadcrumbs again. Place the nuggets on the greased frying basket; fit in the baking tray. Cook for 14-16 minutes, shaking once.

Turkey Pot Pie

Prep + Cook Time: 75 minutes | Serves: 4

Ingredients

¼ cup butter
1 shallot, chopped
1 carrot, chopped
¼ cup flour
1 ½ cups chicken broth
¼ cup heavy cream

1 cup frozen peas
¼ tsp garlic powder
½ tsp mustard powder
½ lb turkey breast, cubed
Salt and black pepper to taste
1 (9-inch) unbaked pie crust

Directions

Preheat Cuisinart on Bake function to 350 F. Melt the butter in a pan over medium heat. Stir-fry the turkey for 3-4 minutes; set aside. Sauté the shallot and carrot in the pan until tender, 4-5 minutes. Sprinkle the flour over and stir with a whisk for 1 minute. Gradually add the broth, whisking constantly until slightly thickened. Return the turkey and simmer for 6-8 minutes.

Stir in the heavy cream and peas for 1 more minute. Season with garlic powder, mustard powder, salt, and pepper. Pour the mix into a 9-inch baking dish and lay the pie crust on top. Seal edges with a fork, trimming any excess. Cut slits in several places on the top crust. Cook for 45-50 minutes until the pastry is golden. When cooking is complete, remove the pan from the oven. The crust should be golden brown and the filling bubbling. Serve.

MEAT RECIPES

Italian Pork Skewers

Prep + Cook Time: 25 minutes | Serves: 4

Ingredients

3 tsp olive oil
1 lb pork tenderloin, cut into 1-inch cubes
2 zucchini, cut crosswise into rounds
1 red bell pepper, cut into 1-inch squares

2 tsp Italian seasoning
1 tsp ground cumin
1 lemon, zested and cut into wedges
2 tbsp basil leaves, chiffonade

Directions

Preheat Cuisinart on Bake function to 380 F. Place the pork cubes, zucchini, bell pepper, Italian seasoning, cumin, lemon zest, and 2 tbsp of olive oil in a large bowl and toss well to coat.

Thread the pork and vegetables alternately onto 8 skewers. Transfer them on a greased baking tray and cook for 14-16 minutes, turning over a couple of times or until cooked through. Sprinkle the skewers with basil. Serve with lemon wedges on the side.

Sweet-Dijon Pork Chops

Prep + Cook Time: 20 minutes | Serves: 3

Ingredients

3 pork chops, ½-inch thick
Salt and black pepper to taste
1 tbsp maple syrup

1 ½ tbsp minced garlic
3 tbsp Dijon mustard

Directions

In a bowl, add maple syrup, garlic, mustard, salt, and pepper and mix well. Add in the pork and toss to coat. Put it into the greased basket and fit in the baking tray. Cook in your Cuisinart at 350 F for 6 minutes on Air Fry function. Flip the chops with a spatula and cook further for 6 minutes. Once ready, remove them to a platter and serve with steamed asparagus if desired.

Cajun Pork Strips

Prep + Cook Time: 30 minutes + marinating time | Serves: 4

Ingredients

1 pound Boston butt, sliced across the grain into 2-inch-long strips
2 tbsp olive oil   Salt and black pepper to taste

2 large eggs
1 tbsp flour

1 cup breadcrumbs
1 tsp Cajun seasoning

Directions

In a bowl, place olive oil, salt, and pepper and mix well. Stir in the pork, cover, and let it marinate for 15 minutes. Preheat Cuisinart on Air Fry function to 400 F.

Beat the eggs in a shallow bowl. Mix the flour and Cajun seasoning in another bowl. Add the breadcrumbs to a deep plate. Dredge the pork in the flour, then in the eggs, followed by the breadcrumbs. Place in the greased cooking basket and fit in the baking tray. Cook for 20 minutes, shaking once. Serve warm.

Pork Meatballs with Cheese

Prep + Cook Time: 25 minutes | Serves: 4

Ingredients

1 ½ lb ground pork
1 large onion, chopped
½ tsp maple syrup

2 tsp Dijon mustard
Salt and black pepper to taste
2 tbsp grated Cheddar cheese

Directions

In a bowl, add ground pork, onion, maple syrup, mustard, salt, pepper, and cheddar cheese and mix well. Use your hands to form small balls.

Place in the fryer basket and fit in the baking tray; cook in your Cuisinart at 400 F for 10 minutes on Air Fry function. Shake and cook further for 5 minutes. Remove them onto a wire rack and serve with zoodles and marinara sauce if desired.

Almond & Apple Pork Balls

Prep + Cook Time: 45 minutes | Serves: 4

Ingredients

16 oz pork sausage meat
1 whole egg, beaten
1 onion, chopped

2 tbsp ground almonds
Salt and black pepper to taste
1 small apple, peeled and grated

Directions

Preheat Cuisinart oven to 350 F on Air Fry function. In a bowl, mix the pork sausage meat, onion, almonds, apple, egg, pepper, and salt. Mix to coat well and set aside for 15 minutes.

Form balls from the mixture and add them to the greased frying basket. Fit in the baking tray and cook for 25 minutes, shaking once, until golden and cooked through. Serve warm.

Tamarind Pork Chops with Green Beans

Prep + Cook Time: 40 minutes + marinating time | Serves: 4

Ingredients

1 tbsp olive oil
2 tbsp tamarind paste
1 tbsp garlic, minced
3 tbsp corn syrup
2 tbsp molasses
4 tbsp southwest seasoning

½ tbsp ketchup
½ lb green beans, trimmed
4 pork chops
½ cup green mole sauce
Salt and black pepper to taste

Directions

In a bowl, mix all the ingredients, except for the green beans, pork chops, and mole sauce. Add in 2 tbsp of water. Let the pork chops marinate in the mixture for 30 minutes. Place pork chops in the basket and fit in the baking tray; cook for 25 minutes on Air Fry function at 350 F.

Blanch the green beans in salted water until crisp-tender, 2-3 minutes. Using a slotted spoon, transfer them to an ice bath and chill for 2 minutes. Drain and season with salt and pepper. Drizzle the pork with mole sauce and serve with green beans on the side.

Mushroom-Stuffed Pork

Prep + Cook Time: 45 minutes | Serves: 4

Ingredients

2 tbsp olive oil
1 ½ lb pork tenderloin
Salt and black pepper to taste
½ tsp dried oregano

1 shallot, chopped
1 cup mushrooms, chopped
2 garlic cloves, minced
2 tbsp sage leaves, chopped

Directions

Heat the olive oil in a saucepan over medium heat and stir-fry the shallot, garlic, and mushrooms until tender, about 5 minutes. Season with salt, pepper, oregano, and sage.

Slice down the long end of the tenderloin and open it like a book. Cover with plastic wrap and pound it to ½-inch thickness using a meat mallet. Season with salt and pepper. Spread the mushroom mixture evenly over the pork and roll up tightly, securing the ends with toothpicks.

Preheat Cuisinart oven to 350 F on bake function. Place the pork into the greased cooking basket and fit in the baking tray. Cook for 20-25 minutes, turning once or twice. Let the pork sit for a few minutes before slicing. Serve and enjoy!

Teriyaki Pork Ribs

Prep + Cook Time: 40 minutes + marinating time| Serves: 3

Ingredients

1 tbsp olive oil
1 pound pork ribs
Salt and black pepper to taste
1 tbsp sugar
1 tsp ginger puree

1 tsp five-spice powder
1 tbsp teriyaki sauce
1 tbsp soy sauce
1 garlic clove, minced

Directions

In a bowl, mix salt, pepper, sugar, ginger puree, five-spice powder, and teriyaki sauce. Add in pork ribs and let sit for 2 hours in the refrigerator.

Preheat Cuisinart oven to 350 F on Air Fry function. Remove the ribs, place them in the greased basket and fit in the baking tray. Cook for 30 minutes, turning once until the ribs are browned.

Heat olive oil In a pan over medium heat and fry the garlic for 30 seconds. Pour in the sauce and cook for a few minutes until the sauce has slightly thickened. Adjust the seasoning. Pour the sauce over the warm ribs and serve immediately. Enjoy!

Herby Pork Burgers

Prep + Cook Time: 25 minutes | Serves: 4

Ingredients

1 pound ground pork
1 large egg
1 tbsp fresh parsley, chopped
1 tsp fresh thyme, chopped
½ tsp garlic powder
Salt and black pepper to taste

4 hamburger buns, halved
¼ cup mayonnaise
1 tomato, cut into slices
½ English cucumber, sliced
½ red onion, thinly sliced
½ cup Romaine lettuce, shredded

Directions

Preheat your Cuisinart to 350 F on Bake function. Add the ground pork, egg, parsley, thyme, garlic powder, salt, and pepper to a bowl and mix well. Roll the mixture into 4 balls; flatten them using your hands to make 4 burgers. Fit the frying basket in the baking tray.

Add in the burgers and spritz them with cooking spray. Cook for 8 minutes, flip, then cook for an additional 7-8 minutes. Place the patties on the buns' bottoms, add mayonnaise, tomato, cucumber, onion, and lettuce on top, and cover with the bun tops. Serve and enjoy!

Cheddar & Bacon Pork Sliders

Prep + Cook Time: 30 minutes | Serves: 2

Ingredients

2 pork boneless pork chops
1 tsp pork seasoning
Salt and black pepper to taste
4 thick bacon slices

1 cup grated Cheddar cheese
½ tbsp Worcestershire sauce
2 bread buns, halved

Directions

Preheat Cuisinart on Bake function to 380 F. Place the pork in the baking pan and season with pepper, salt, and pork seasoning; drizzle with Worcestershire sauce. Cook for 10 minutes, turn, top with bacon, and cook for 5 more minutes until the bacon is crispy. Remove and sprinkle with cheddar cheese. Return and bake for 3-4 minutes until the cheese melts. Place the meat into the halved buns and serve with tomato dip if desired.

Carolina-Style BBQ Ribs

Prep + Cook Time: 45 minutes | Serves: 4

Ingredients

2 lb pork baby back ribs, silver skin removed
1 tsp Worcestershire sauce
2 tbsp light brown sugar
1 tsp ancho chili powder

1 tsp ground mustard seed
Salt and black pepper to taste
1 cup Carolina BBQ Sauce

Directions

Preheat your Cuisinart to 380 F on Air Fry function. Remove the membrane from the bone side of the ribs and cut them into small pieces. Mix the Worcestershire sauce, brown sugar, chili powder, and mustard, then rub the mixture onto the ribs on all sides. Season to taste.

Fit the greased fryer basket in the baking tray. Place the ribs in the basket, even if they touch. Cook for about 18 minutes, turn, then cook for another 15-18 minutes until crispy. Coat the ribs with Carolina BBQ Sauce. Serve hot.

Spinach-Based Pesto Pork Chops

Prep + Cook Time: 30 minutes + marinating time | Serves: 2

Ingredients

¼ cup olive oil
2 boneless pork loin chops
1 tbsp fresh lemon juice

1 garlic clove, minced
1 cup baby spinach
½ cup Pecorino cheese, grated

Directions

Blend lemon juice, garlic, spinach, cheese, and 1 tbsp of water in your food processor or blender until roughly chopped. Slowly pour in the olive oil while the machine is running until smooth.

Preheat your Cuisinart to 370 F on Air Fry function. Coat the chops with the pesto and let it marinate for 20 minutes. Fit the fryer basket in the baking tray. Place the chops on the basket. Cook for 8 minutes, flip, then cook for another 7 minutes. When the time is up, the chops should be browned. Allow the meat to sit for 5 minutes. Serve warm.

Italian Beef Pot Roast

Prep + Cook Time: 90 minutes | Serves: 4

Ingredients

2 tbsp olive oil
1 tsp garlic powder
½ tsp porcini mushroom powder
½ tsp Italian seasoning

1 tbsp fresh thyme, chopped
1 tbsp fresh rosemary, chopped
Salt and black pepper to taste
1 (1 ½-pound) beef rump roast

Directions

Preheat your Cuisinart to 360 F on Bake function. Place the beef in a Ziploc bag. Combine the olive oil, garlic powder, porcini powder, Italian seasoning, thyme, rosemary, salt, and pepper in a bowl and mix well. Pour the mixture over the beef and shake to coat on all sides.

Remove the beef and place it on the greased baking tray. Cook for 65-70 minutes or until browned and the internal temperature is around 165 F on an instant-read thermometer. Allow the roast to cool for 5-10 minutes. Slice the roast and serve warm.

Grandma's Ground Beef Balls

Prep + Cook Time: 25 minutes | Serves: 4

Ingredients

1 tbsp olive oil
1 ½ pounds ground beef
1 large red onion, chopped

1 tsp garlic, minced
2 whole eggs, beaten
Salt and black pepper to taste

Directions

Place a skillet over medium heat and warm the oil. Add in onion and garlic and sauté for 3 minutes until tender. Remove to a bowl to cool. Add in the ground beef and eggs and mix well.

Season with salt and pepper. Roll the mixture into golf-sized balls and place them in the greased frying basket. Fit in the baking tray and cook in your Cuisinart for 15-18 minutes on Air Fry function at 350 F, turning once or twice. Serve and enjoy!

Classic Glazed Beef Meatloaf

Prep + Cook Time: 70 minutes | Serves: 4

Ingredients

1 ½ pounds ground beef
1 potato, peeled and shredded
1 tbsp Dijon mustard
1 large egg
1 onion, shredded
2 garlic cloves, minced
¼ cup milk

1 tsp allspice
Salt and black pepper to taste
½ cup ketchup
½ tsp Worcestershire sauce
1 tbsp dark brown sugar
1 tsp apple cider vinegar

Directions

Preheat your Cuisinart to 380 F on Bake function. Thoroughly combine the ground beef, potato, mustard, egg, onion, garlic, milk, allspice, salt, and pepper in a bowl. Shape the mixture into a loaf. Cook the loaf for 40 minutes until the meat reaches an internal temperature of 165 F.

While the loaf is cooking, combine the ketchup, brown sugar, Worcestershire sauce, and vinegar in a bowl. When the time is up, take the loaf out and smear the ketchup mix on top evenly. Cook for another 15-20 minutes. The loaf should have an internal temp of 165°F. Serve warm.

Hot Flank Steak with Mexican Salsa

Prep + Cook Time: 40 minutes | Serves: 4

Ingredients

1 tbsp olive oil
1 ½ lb beef flank steak
1 tsp garlic powder
1 tsp Ancho chili powder
2 large tomatoes, chopped
1 cup canned corn

½ avocado, chopped
¼ red onion, chopped
1 tbsp Poblano pepper, chopped
1 tbsp fresh cilantro, chopped
Salt and black pepper to taste

Directions

Preheat Cuisinart oven to 450 F on Broil function. Sprinkle the steaks with garlic powder, Ancho chili powder, salt, and pepper and drizzle with olive oil. Put them into the fryer basket and fit in the baking tray. Broil for 10 minutes, flip, then broil for another 10 minutes. When cooking is complete, the steak should be browned and reach an internal temperature of around 140 F for medium-rare. Allow the steak to cool for 10 minutes, then slice it thinly against the grain.

Add the tomato, corn, avocado, onion, Poblano pepper, and cilantro to a bowl and stir, then season with salt and pepper. Serve the beef warm with Mexican salsa on the side.

Country-Fried Steak with Creamy Gravy

Prep + Cook Time: 30 minutes | Serves: 2

Ingredients

2 tbsp butter
1 cup flour
1 tsp garlic powder
1 tsp shallot powder
1 tsp smoked paprika
¼ tsp mustard powder
½ tsp dried sage, crushed

2 large eggs
2 top round steaks
Salt and black pepper to taste
2 tbsp cornflour
1 ½ cups milk
¼ cup heavy cream

Directions

Preheat your Cuisinart to 380 F on Air Fry function. Combine the flour, garlic powder, shallot powder, smoked paprika, mustard powder, and sage in a bowl and mix well. In a different bowl, whisk the eggs. Sprinkle the steaks with salt and pepper, then dip them in the eggs.

Coat them in the flour mixture. Shake the steaks off of excess flour and spritz with cooking spray. Put the steaks into the greased fryer basket and fit in the baking tray. Cook for 9 minutes, then flip, and spritz with more cooking spray and cook for 7 more minutes.

As the meat is cooking, put a skillet over medium heat and melt the butter. Mix the cornflour with the milk in a small bowl, then add it slowly to the skillet, stirring continuously for about 5 minutes, or until the gravy is creamy, uniform, and smooth. Lastly, stir in the heavy cream. Adjust the seasoning. Top the steaks with the gravy and serve warm.

Beef Rolls with Pesto & Spinach

Prep + Cook Time: 25 minutes | Serves: 4

Ingredients

4 (1/8-inch) thick sirloin steaks
Salt and black pepper to taste
2 tbsp basil pesto

4 mozzarella cheese slices
5 oz spinach leaves
1 bell pepper, deseeded and sliced

Directions

Spread the pesto over the beef steaks. Top with mozzarella cheese, spinach, and bell pepper. Roll the steaks up tightly around the filling and secure the edges with toothpicks. Season with salt and pepper. Place the rolls in the greased basket and fit in the baking tray. Cook in your Cuisinart for 15 minutes on Air Fry function at 400 F, turning once. Serve immediately!

Beef & Rice Stuffed Bell Peppers

Prep + Cook Time: 45 minutes | Serves: 4

Ingredients

2 tbsp olive oil
2 red bell peppers
2 yellow bell peppers
1 pound ground beef
1 shallot, finely chopped
2 garlic cloves, minced

1 cup tomato sauce
½ cup basmati rice
1 tsp dried herbs
½ tsp sweet paprika
Salt and black pepper to taste

Directions

Cook the rice in salted water for 5-8 minutes. Drain and set aside. Cut the tops of the peppers and carefully discard the core and seeds (reserve the tops). Set the peppers aside.

Warm the olive oil in a skillet over medium heat and stir-fry the shallot and garlic for 2 minutes. Add in the ground beef and cook for 5-6 minutes until it is no longer pink. Stir in the paprika, herbs, rice, salt, and pepper for 1 minute. Pour in the tomato sauce and stir. Take the skillet off the heat. Spoon the filling into the peppers evenly and place the tops.

Preheat Cuisinart oven to 350 F on Bake function. Arrange the peppers on a baking dish and cook for 15 minutes, or until the peppers have softened and the tops are charred. Serve hot.

Turkish-Style Lamb Chops

Prep + Cook Time: 30 minutes | Serves: 2

Ingredients

2 tbsp Dijon mustard
1 garlic clove, minced
¼ cup breadcrumbs
1 tsp ground sumac
1 tsp ground cumin

¼ tsp red chili flakes
1 tsp ground coriander
1 lemon, zested
4 lamb loin chops
Salt and black pepper to taste

Directions

Preheat Cuisinart oven to 420 F on Bake function. In a bowl, mix the breadcrumbs, sumac, cumin, red chili flakes, ground coriander, and lemon zest. Thoroughly combine the mustard and garlic in a small bowl. Sprinkle salt and pepper on the lamb chops, brush them with the mustard mix, and coat with the breadcrumb mix.

Lay the chops on a foil-lined baking dish and spritz them with cooking oil. Cook for 15 minutes until well browned and internal temperature registers 130 F on an instant-read thermometer. Allow the lamb to cool for 5 minutes. Serve warm.

FISH & SEAFOOD

Tilapia Tacos

Prep + Cook Time: 30 minutes | Serves: 3

Ingredients

1 pound tilapia, cut into ½-inch strips
1 tsp taco seasoning
½ lime, juiced
½ cup flour
1 large egg
1 cup panko breadcrumbs

6 corn tortillas, warm
5 oz coleslaw mix
1 tbsp cilantro, roughly chopped
1 avocado, sliced
3 tbsp sour cream

Directions

Preheat Cuisinart on Air Fry function to 390 F. Season the tilapia strips with half of the taco seasoning and drizzle with some lime juice. Spread the flour on a plate, whisk the egg in a shallow bowl, and combine the crumbs with the remaining taco seasoning in another bowl.

Dip the fish into the flour, shaking off any excess, then into the egg, and lastly, coat well in the crumbs. Fit the greased fryer basket in the baking tray. Spray the strips with cooking oil and place them into the basket.

Cook in the upper position for 13-16 minutes, turning over halfway through until fork-tender inside and crispy outside. Divide the tilapia strips between the tortillas, top with coleslaw mix, cilantro, avocado, sour cream, and the remaining lime juice. Serve warm.

Easy Salmon Cakes

Prep + Cook Time: 20 minutes + cooling time| Serves: 2

Ingredients

1 cup salmon, cooked
1 potato, cooked and mashed
A handful of capers

1 tbsp dill, chopped
1 lemon, zested
¼ cup plain flour

Directions

Carefully flake the salmon in a bowl. Stir in zest, capers, dill, and mashed potato. Shape the mixture into cakes and dust them with flour. Place in the fridge for 60 minutes.

Preheat your Cuisinart to 350 F on Air Fry function. Remove the cakes from the fridge and arrange them in the greased basket. Fit in the baking tray and cook for 10 minutes, shaking once halfway through. Serve warm or chilled.

Simple Lemon Salmon

Prep + Cook Time: 15 minutes | Serves: 2

Ingredients

2 salmon fillets
Salt to taste

1 lemon, zested

Directions

Preheat Cuisinart on Air Fry function to 360 F. Spray the fillets with cooking oil and rub them with salt and lemon zest. Line a baking dish with parchment paper. Cook the fillets in your Cuisinart for 10 minutes, turning halfway through the cooking time. Serve and enjoy!

Festive Salmon Kebabs

Prep + Cook Time: 25 minutes | Serves: 4

Ingredients

2 tbsp sesame oil
1 lb salmon fillets, cut into 1-inch cubes
Salt to taste

¼ cup honey
1-inch fresh ginger, grated
2 tbsp cilantro leaves, chiffonade

Directions

Preheat Cuisinart on Bake function to 350 F. Salt the salmon cubes and thread them onto skewers. Place them into the greased fryer basket and fit in the baking tray. Blend the sesame oil, ginger, and honey in a small bowl. Smear the salmon kebabs with the mixture. Bake for 12-14 minutes, turning them over halfway through the cooking time. Serve topped with cilantro.

Baked Sole with Fennel & Cherry Tomatoes

Prep + Cook Time: 35 minutes | Serves: 2

Ingredients

2 tbsp olive oil
2 sole fillets
Salt to taste
1 carrot, cut into strips
½ lb baby potatoes, thinly sliced
1 red onion, sliced into wedges

1 garlic clove, finely sliced
¼ bulb fennel, finely sliced
10 cherry tomatoes, halved
1 tbsp fresh dill, chopped
½ tsp red chili flakes

Directions

Preheat Cuisinart on Air Fry function to 350 F. Place the potatoes and carrot into the fryer basket and fit in the baking tray. Toss them with salt and some olive oil. Cook for 10 minutes.

Place onion, fennel, garlic, tomatoes, salt, and some oil in a bowl; toss to coat. Spread the veggies over the potatoes and carrot. Top with the sole and drizzle with the remaining olive oil; season.

Scatter the chili flakes all over the sole fillets and place them in the Cuisinart. Cook for 8-12 minutes until the fish is golden brown and the vegetables are tender. Sprinkle with dill and serve.

Almond-Crusted Flounder Fillets

Prep + Cook Time: 25 minutes | Serves: 4

Ingredients

4 flounder fillets
Salt and black pepper to taste
1 cup almonds, ground

½ cup panko breadcrumbs
1 large egg
1 lemon, cut into wedges

Directions

Preheat Cuisinart on Air Fry function to 380 F. Mix the almonds and breadcrumbs in a bowl. Whisk the egg with salt and pepper until well blended in a separate bowl.

Dip the flounder fillets into the egg mix, let the excess drip off, then roll them in the nut mix. Transfer to the fryer basket and fit in the baking tray.

Spritz the fish with cooking spray on both sides. Cook for 12 minutes, or until browned and crunchy. Flip the fish at about 6 minutes, so both sides are equally cooked. Serve warm with lemon wedges on the side.

Savory Cod Fish in Soy Sauce

Prep + Cook Time: 30 minutes | Serves: 4

Ingredients

3 tbsp olive oil
4 cod fish fillets
1 tsp ground coriander
Salt to taste
2 green onions, chopped

1 cup water
4 ginger slices
2 tbsp light soy sauce
1 tsp dark soy sauce
4 cubes rock sugar

Directions

Sprinkle the cod with salt and coriander and drizzle with olive oil. Place in the cooking basket and fit in the baking tray; cook for 15 minutes at 360 F on Air Fry function, flipping once.

Place the remaining ingredients in a frying pan over medium heat and cook for 5 minutes until the sauce reaches desired consistency. Pour the sauce over the fish and serve.

Cheesy Tilapia Fillets

Prep + Cook Time: 15 minutes | Serves: 4

Ingredients

1 tbsp olive oil
¾ cup grated Parmesan cheese
2 tsp paprika

1 tbsp chopped parsley
¼ tsp garlic powder
4 tilapia fillets

Directions

Preheat Cuisinart on Air Fry function to 350 F. Mix parsley, Parmesan cheese, garlic, and paprika in a bowl. Brush the olive oil over the fillets and then coat with the Parmesan mixture. Place the tilapia onto a lined baking sheet and cook for 8-10 minutes, turning once. Serve.

Golden Cod Nuggets

Prep + Cook Time: 25 minutes | Serves: 4

Ingredients

1 tbsp olive oil
1 ¼ lb cod fillets, cut into 4 to 6 chunks each
½ cup flour

1 egg
1 cup cornflakes
Salt and black pepper to taste

Directions

Blitz the cornflakes in a blender until crumbed. Season the fish chunks with salt and pepper. In a bowl, beat the egg along with 1 tbsp of water. Dredge the chunks in flour first, then dip in the egg, and finally coat with cornflakes. Arrange the fish pieces on a parchment-lined sheet. Brush with olive oil. Cook in your Cuisinart on Air Fry at 350 F for 15 minutes until crispy. Serve.

Garlic-Butter Haddock

Prep + Cook Time: 25 minutes | Serves: 2

Ingredients

2 tbsp butter, melted
2 haddock fillets
2 tsp blackening seasoning

1 lime, juiced
1 garlic clove, mashed
2 tbsp cilantro, chopped

Directions

In a bowl, blend the garlic, lime juice, cilantro, and butter until the sauce reaches your desired consistency. Pour half of the sauce over the fillets and sprinkle with blackening seasoning. Place the fillets into the basket and fit in the baking tray; cook for 15 minutes at 360 F on Air Fry function, flipping once. Serve the fish drizzled with the remaining sauce.

Delightful Catfish Fillets

Prep + Cook Time: 25 minutes | Serves: 4

Ingredients

4 catfish fillets
¼ cup seasoned fish fry

1 tbsp parsley, chopped

Directions

Add seasoned fish fry and catfish fillets in a large Ziploc bag and massage well to coat. Place the fillets in your fryer basket and fit in the baking tray; cook in your Cuisinart for 10 minutes at 360 F on Air Fry function. Flip the fish and cook for 2-3 more minutes. Top with parsley to serve.

Effortless Coconut Shrimp

Prep + Cook Time: 15 minutes | Serves: 3

Ingredients

1 pound shrimp
½ cup flour
1 large egg, beaten

1 cup panko breadcrumbs
½ cup shredded coconut
½ cup sweet chili sauce

Directions

Preheat Cuisinart on Air Fry function to 375 F. Place the flour and egg in 2 different bowls. Mix breadcrumbs and coconut in a third bowl. Roll the shrimp in the flour, then shake off.

Dip in the egg and then coat well in the coconut mixture. Place the shrimp in the greased fryer basket and fit in the baking tray. Spritz the shrimp with cooking oil on both sides. Cook in the upper position for about 5 minutes per side, or until golden brown and crispy. Serve with sweet chili sauce on the side.

Chili-Rubbed Jumbo Shrimp

Prep + Cook Time: 10 minutes | Serves: 4

Ingredients

1 tbsp olive oil
1 ¼ lb jumbo shrimp
Salt to taste

¼ tsp old bay seasoning
⅓ tsp smoked paprika
¼ tsp chili powder

Directions

Preheat Cuisinart on Air Fry function to 390 F. In a bowl, add the shrimp, paprika, olive oil, salt, old bay seasoning, and chili powder; mix well. Place the shrimp in the basket and fit in the baking tray. Cook for 5 minutes, flipping once. Serve with mayo and rice if desired.

Rosemary Buttered Prawns

Prep + Cook Time: 15 minutes + marinating time| Serves: 2

Ingredients

½ tbsp melted butter
½ lb large prawns

1 rosemary sprig, chopped
Salt and black pepper to taste

Directions

Combine butter, rosemary, salt, and pepper in a bowl. Add in the prawns and mix to coat. Cover the bowl and refrigerate for 1 hour.

Preheat Cuisinart on Air Fry function to 350 F. Remove the prawns from the fridge and place them in the basket. Fit in the baking tray and cook for 10 minutes, flipping once. Serve.

Speedy Fried Scallops

Prep + Cook Time: 10 minutes | Serves: 4

Ingredients

12 fresh scallops
3 tbsp flour

1 egg, lightly beaten
1 cup breadcrumbs

Directions

Coat the scallops with flour. Dip into the egg, then into the breadcrumbs. Spray with cooking oil and arrange them on the basket. Fit in the baking tray and cook for 6 minutes at 360 F on Air Fry function, turning once halfway through cooking. Serve.

Scallops with Orange Glaze

Prep + Cook Time: 15 minutes | Serves: 4

Ingredients

1 pound jumbo sea scallops
1 tbsp soy sauce
2 tbsp orange juice
1 tsp orange zest

½ tsp parsley flakes
1 tbsp butter, melted
2 tbsp dry white wine
Salt and black pepper to taste

Directions

Preheat Cuisinart on Air Fry function to 400 F. In a bowl, mix soy sauce, orange sauce, orange zest, white wine, salt, and pepper. Add in the scallops and toss to coat. Let sit for 10 minutes.

Lightly grease the frying basket with cooking oil. Brush the scallops with buttes and sprinkle with parsley. Place them in the basket and fit it in the baking tray. Cook for 8-10 minutes, shaking halfway through the cooking time. Serve and enjoy!

Crispy Crab Legs

Prep + Cook Time: 15 minutes | Serves: 4

Ingredients

½ cup butter, melted

3 pounds crab legs

Directions

Preheat Cuisinart on Air Fry function to 380 F. Cover the crab legs with salted water and let them stay for a few minutes. Drain, pat them dry and place the legs in the basket. Fit in the baking tray and brush with some butter; cook for 10 minutes, flipping once. Drizzle with the remaining butter and serve.

Lemon-Garlic Butter Lobster

Prep + Cook Time: 15 minutes | Serves: 2

Ingredients

1 tbsp butter

4 oz lobster tails

1 tsp garlic, minced

Salt and black pepper to taste

½ tbsp lemon Juice

Directions

Add all the ingredients to a food processor except for lobster and blend well. Wash lobster and halve using a meat knife; clean the skin of the lobster and cover with the marinade.

Preheat your Cuisinart to 380 F on Air Fry function. Place the lobster in the cooking basket and fit in the baking tray; cook for 10 minutes. Serve with fresh herbs.

Delicious Fried Seafood Mix

Prep + Cook Time: 20 minutes | Serves: 4

Ingredients

1 lb fresh scallops, mussels, fish fillets, prawns, shrimp

2 eggs, lightly beaten

Salt and black pepper to taste

1 cup breadcrumbs mixed with the zest of 1 lemon

Directions

Dip each piece of the seafood into the eggs and season with salt and pepper. Coat in the crumbs and spray with cooking oil. Arrange on the frying basket and fit in the baking tray; cook for 10 minutes at 400 F on Air Fry function, turning once halfway through. Serve.

MEATLESS RECIPES

Collard Greens Chips

Prep + Cook Time: 15 minutes | Serves: 4

Ingredients

1 tbsp olive oil
½ tsp chili powder

10 oz collard greens, thick stems removed
Sea salt flakes to taste

Directions

Preheat Cuisinart on Air Fry function to 360 F. Cut the collard green leaves into similar-sized pieces. Coat with olive oil and chili powder. In batches, spread out over the greased fryer basket and fit in the baking tray. Fry for 5 minutes, flipping halfway through cooking to ensure even crisping. Repeat with the rest of the collard greens. Sprinkle with salt and serve.

Ratatouille-Style Fries

Prep + Cook Time: 45 minutes | Serves: 4

Ingredients

½ cup olive oil
1 large eggplant
4 potatoes, peeled

3 zucchinis
½ cup cornstarch
Salt to taste

Directions

Preheat Cuisinart on Air Fry function to 390 F. Cut the eggplant, potatoes, and zucchini into ½-inch strips about 3 inches long. In a bowl, stir the cornstarch, ½ cup of water, salt, ~~pepper~~, oil, eggplant, zucchini, and potatoes. Place one-third of the veggie strips in the basket

Fit in the baking tray; cook for 12 minutes, shaking once. Once ready, transfer them to a serving platter. Repeat the cooking process for the remaining veggie strips. Serve warm.

Crispy Fried Green Beans

Prep + Cook Time: 25 minutes | Serves: 4

Ingredients

1 cup panko breadcrumbs
2 whole eggs, beaten
½ cup Parmesan cheese, grated
½ cup flour

1 tsp cayenne pepper
1 ½ pounds green beans
Salt and black pepper to taste

Directions

In a bowl, mix panko breadcrumbs, Parmesan cheese, cayenne pepper, salt, and pepper. Roll the green beans in the flour and dip them into the eggs. Dredge them in the parmesan-panko mix. Place the prepared beans in the greased cooking basket and fit in the baking tray; cook for 15 minutes on Air Fry function at 350 F, shaking once. Serve and enjoy!

Sweet & Spicy Brussels Sprouts

Prep + Cook Time: 40 minutes | Serves: 3

Ingredients

1 lb Brussels sprouts, trimmed, halved
Salt to taste
2 tbsp honey

2 tsp hot sauce
1 tsp fresh lemon juice

Directions

Stir together the honey, hot sauce, and lemon juice in a mixing bowl; set aside. Preheat your Cuisinart on Air Fry function to 300 F. Lightly coat the fryer basket with cooking spray and fit in the baking tray. Spread the halved sprouts on the basket and season with salt.

Spritz lightly with cooking spray. Cook in the upper position for 18-20 minutes, shaking the basket occasionally. Increase temperature to 350 F and cook for a further 10-12 minutes or until crisp-tender. Toss the Brussels sprouts in the prepared sauce and serve immediately.

Sweet Potato Fries with Sriracha Dip

Prep + Cook Time: 30 minutes | Serves: 4

Ingredients

3 tbsp olive oil
½ tsp salt
½ tsp garlic powder
½ tsp chili powder
¼ tsp cumin

4 sweet potatoes, cut into thick strips
¼ cup sour cream
1 tsp Sriracha sauce
½ cup light mayonnaise

Directions

In a small bowl, combine the sour cream, mayonnaise, and sriracha sauce. Mix with a fork until creamy. Keep in the refrigerator until ready to serve.

Preheat Cuisinart on Air Fry function to 380 F. In a bowl, mix salt, garlic powder, chili, cumin, and olive oil. Coat the strips well in the mixture and arrange them on the basket without overcrowding. Fit in the baking tray and cook in your Cuisinart for 20 minutes or until crispy. Serve warm with the sriracha dip on the side.

Maple-Baked Borlotti Beans

Prep + Cook Time: 70 minutes | Serves: 4

Ingredients

3 (15-ounce) cans Borlotti beans, drained
1 shallot, chopped
Celery salt to taste
½ cup vegetable broth
½ cup tomato paste

¼ cup maple syrup
1 tbsp whole-grain mustard
1 garlic clove, minced
2 tbsp scallions, chopped

Directions

Preheat your Cuisinart to 350 F on Bake function. Spritz a baking dish with cooking spray, then add the beans, shallot, broth, tomato paste, maple syrup, mustard, and garlic. Sprinkle with celery salt. Cover and seal the dish with aluminum foil and cook for 50-55 minutes. Discard the foil and bake for 5 more minutes. When cooking is complete, the beans should be soft and the sauce thickened. Sprinkle with scallions and serve warm.

Authentic Pizza Margherita

Prep + Cook Time: 25 minutes | Serves: 4

Ingredients

1 pound pizza dough, thawed
½ cup marinara sauce
2 tbsp Parmesan cheese, grated
3 ounces fresh mozzarella, thinly sliced

½ tsp dried oregano
2 tbsp basil leaves, thinly sliced
6 black olives

Directions

Preheat Cuisinart on Bake function to 390 F. Stretch your dough on a lightly greased baking pan. Spread with a thin layer of marinara sauce, allowing a 1-inch border.

Scatter with the oregano and Parmesan cheese and top with the mozzarella cheese. Bake the pizza in the lower position for 12-14 minutes, or until the cheese melts and the edges of the pizza are golden. Garnish with basil and olives. Serve sliced. Enjoy!

Chipotle Beet & Kale Crisps

Prep + Cook Time: 35 minutes | Serves: 4

Ingredients

2 tbsp vegetable oil
½ tsp chipotle chili powder
1 beet, peeled and thinly sliced

1 bunch of kale leaves, thick stems removed
Salt to taste

Directions

Preheat Cuisinart on Air Fry function to 360 F. Cut the kale leaves into 1.5-inch strips. Transfer to the fryer basket and fit in the baking tray. Add the sliced beet to the basket and spread the vegetables out, spacing them apart. Toss the vegetable with oil, chipotle chili powder, and salt. Work in batches if necessary. Cook for 8-12 minutes, turning once until crisp. Serve chilled.

Herby Tofu

Prep + Cook Time: 30 minutes | Serves: 2

Ingredients

6 oz extra firm tofu
Black pepper to taste
1 tbsp vegetable broth
1 tbsp soy sauce

⅓ tsp dried oregano
⅓ tsp garlic powder
⅓ tsp dried basil
⅓ tsp onion powder

Directions

Place the tofu on a cutting board and cut it into 3 lengthwise slices with a knife. Line a side of the cutting board with paper towels, place the tofu on it, and cover with a paper towel. Use your hands to press the tofu gently until as much liquid has been extracted from it. Chop the tofu into 8 cubes; set aside.

In another bowl, add the soy sauce, vegetable broth, oregano, basil, garlic powder, onion powder, and black pepper and mix well with a spoon. Rub the spice mixture onto the tofu. Let it marinate for 10 minutes.

Preheat Cuisinart on Air Fry function to 390 F. Place the tofu in the fryer's basket in a single layer and fit in the baking tray. Cook for 10 minutes, flipping it at the 6-minute mark. Remove to a plate and serve with a green salad if desired.

Traditional Jacket Potatoes

Prep + Cook Time: 30 minutes | Serves: 4

Ingredients

1 tsp butter
4 potatoes, well washed
2 garlic cloves, minced

Salt and black pepper to taste
1 tsp rosemary

Directions

Preheat your Cuisinart to 360 F on Air Fry function. Prick the potatoes with a fork. Place them into the fryer basket and fit in the baking tray; cook for 25 minutes. Cut the potatoes in half and top with butter and rosemary; season with salt and pepper. Serve immediately.

Cauliflower Rice with Tofu & Peas

Prep + Cook Time: 30 minutes | Serves: 4

Ingredients

Tofu:
½ block tofu, crumbled
½ cup diced onion
2 tbsp soy sauce

1 tsp turmeric
1 cup diced carrot

Cauliflower:
3 cups cauliflower rice
2 tbsp soy sauce
½ cup chopped broccoli
2 garlic cloves, minced

1 ½ tsp toasted sesame oil
1 tbsp minced ginger
½ cup frozen peas
1 tbsp rice vinegar

Directions

Preheat Cuisinart on Air Fry function to 370 F. Combine all the tofu ingredients in a greased baking dish. Cook for 10 minutes, shaking the dish once.

Meanwhile, place all cauliflower ingredients in a large bowl and mix to combine. Stir the cauliflower mixture in the tofu baking dish, return to the oven, and cook for 12 minutes. Serve.

Roasted Carrots

Prep + Cook Time: 20 minutes | Serves: 4

Ingredients

2 tbsp olive oil
1 lb carrots, julienned

1 tsp cumin seeds
2 tbsp fresh cilantro, chopped

Directions

In a bowl, mix olive oil, carrots, and cumin seeds; stir to coat. Place the carrots into a baking tray and cook in your Cuisinart on Bake function at 350 F for 10-15 minutes until golden. Scatter fresh cilantro over the carrots and serve.

Rosemary Butternut Squash Roast

Prep + Cook Time: 30 minutes | Serves: 2

Ingredients

1 butternut squash
1 tbsp dried rosemary
2 tbsp maple syrup

½ cup goat cheese, crumbled
Salt to taste

Directions

Preheat Cuisinart on Air Fry function to 350 F. Place the squash on a cutting board and peel. Cut in half and remove the seeds and pulp. Slice into wedges and season with salt.

Spray the wedges with cooking spray and sprinkle with rosemary. Place the wedges in the basket without overlapping and fit in the baking tray. Cook for 20 minutes, flipping once halfway through. Serve with maple syrup and goat cheese.

Cheesy Frittata with Vegetables

Prep + Cook Time: 30 minutes | Serves: 3

Ingredients

2 tsp olive oil

1 cup baby spinach

⅓ cup sliced mushrooms

1 zucchini, sliced with a 1-inch thickness

1 small red onion, sliced

1 tbsp chopped chives

2 asparagus, trimmed and sliced thinly

5 eggs, cracked into a bowl

⅓ cup milk

Salt and black pepper to taste

⅓ cup grated Cheddar cheese

⅓ cup crumbled Feta cheese

Directions

Preheat Cuisinart on Bake function to 320 F. Line a baking dish with parchment paper. Mix the beaten eggs with milk, salt, and pepper. Heat olive oil in a skillet over medium heat and stir-fry the asparagus, zucchini, onion, mushrooms, and baby spinach for 5 minutes.

Pour the veggies into the baking dish and top with the egg mixture. Sprinkle with feta and cheddar cheeses. Cook in your Cuisinart for 15 minutes. Garnish with chives.

Tasty Polenta Crisps

Prep + Cook Time: 25 minutes + chilling time | Serves: 4

Ingredients

2 cups milk

1 cup instant polenta

Salt and black pepper to taste

Directions

Fill a saucepan with milk and 2 cups of water and place over low heat. Bring to a simmer. Keep whisking as you pour in the polenta. Continue to whisk until polenta thickens and bubbles; season to taste. Add polenta to a lined with parchment paper baking tray and spread out.

Refrigerate for 45 minutes. Slice the polenta into batons and spray with olive oil. Arrange the polenta strips into the basket and fit in the baking tray; cook for 16 minutes at 380 F on Air Fry function, turning once halfway through. Make sure the fries are golden and crispy. Serve.

Chickpea & Carrot Balls

Prep + Cook Time: 30 minutes | Serves: 3

Ingredients

2 tbsp olive oil

2 tbsp soy sauce

1 tbsp flax meal

2 cups cooked chickpeas

½ cup sweet onions

½ cup grated carrots

½ cup roasted cashews

Juice of 1 lemon

½ tsp turmeric

1 tsp cumin

1 tsp garlic powder

1 cup rolled oats

Directions

Combine the olive oil, onions, and carrots into the Air Fryer baking pan and cook them on Air Fry function for 6 minutes at 350 F. Ground the oats and cashews in a food processor. Place in a large bowl. Mix in the chickpeas, lemon juice, and soy sauce. Add in the onions and carrots and the remaining ingredients; mix until fully incorporated. Make meatballs out of the mixture. Increase the temperature to 370 F and cook for 12 minutes, shaking once the basket. Serve.

Yummy Black Bean & Veggie Burritos

Prep + Cook Time: 30 minutes | Serves: 3

Ingredients

3 tsp olive oil

2 green onions, sliced

1 cup chopped red bell peppers

1 jalapeño pepper, minced

½ tsp cumin

½ tsp chili powder

1 can (8 oz) black beans

½ cup canned diced tomatoes

1 cup sweet corn kernels

6 tortillas, warm

½ cup grated cheddar cheese

Salt and black pepper to taste

¼ cup salsa

¼ cup sour cream

1 tbsp cilantro, chopped

Directions

Preheat Cuisinart on Bake function to 350 F. Warm the olive oil in a large nonstick skillet over medium heat and sauté the green onion, jalapeño, and bell pepper for 3-4 minutes. Stir in cumin and chili powder for 30 seconds. Add in the black beans and tomatoes; simmer for 5 minutes. Mix in the corn and season with salt and pepper.

Divide the mixture between the tortillas. Top with cheese, sour cream, and cilantro. Fold the sides of the tortillas over the filling, making the burritos. Place them into the greased fryer basket and fit in the baking tray. Cook for 10-12 minutes, turning them over halfway through the cooking time. Slice in half and serve with the salsa on the side. Enjoy!

Mediterranean Quiche

Prep + Cook Time: 65 minutes | Serves: 4

Ingredients

1 purchased refrigerated pie crust
½ lb broccoli florets, chopped
5 fresh eggs
½ cup heavy cream
¾ cup mozzarella cheese, grated

Salt and black pepper to taste
10 cherry tomatoes, quartered
1 green onion, finely chopped
½ tbsp fresh oregano, chopped
½ tbsp fresh basil, chopped

Directions

Preheat Cuisinart on Bake function to 350 F.

In a large saucepan, boil the broccoli for 2-3 minutes until they are bright green. Drain and set aside to cool. Fit the pie crust in a round cake pan. Cut the edges until even and flute. Whisk the eggs with salt and pepper until well blended. Gently stir in heavy cream and half of the cheese.

Place the broccoli, tomatoes, and green onion into the crust, then add the egg mix on top. Sprinkle with the rest of the cheese, oregano, and basil. Cook for 45-50 minutes until the quiche is puffy and brown, and a toothpick inserted comes out dry and clean. Serve sliced.

Couscous-Stuffed Zucchini

Prep + Cook Time: 65 minutes | Serves: 4

Ingredients

2 tsp olive oil
½ cup couscous
2 large zucchini
1 large tomato, chopped
1 scallion, chopped
½ jalapeño pepper, minced

½ cup corn kernels
1 tbsp fresh cilantro, chopped
1 garlic clove, minced
1 tsp ground cumin
¼ tsp chili powder
½ cup mozzarella cheese, grated

Directions

Cover the couscous with 1 ½ cups of salted boiling water, cover, and let it sit for 5-6 minutes until the water is absorbed. Preheat Cuisinart on Toast function to 400 F. Lay parchment paper on the baking tray. Slice the zucchini in half lengthwise. Make a hollow boat by spooning the insides out. Leave ¼-inch of flesh in the shell. Rub some oil on both sides of the zucchini boats and place them on a cookie sheet.

Combine the couscous, tomato, scallion, jalapeño, corn, cilantro, garlic, cumin, and chili powder in a bowl, then evenly add the mix to the zucchini boats. Sprinkle with cheese. Cook for 45-50 minutes, or until the zucchini is soft and the cheese is melted and brown. Serve hot.

Mom's Blooming Onion

Prep + Cook Time: 30 minutes | Serves: 3

Ingredients

1 large sweet onion
½ cup flour
1 large egg, lightly beaten
2 tbsp milk
½ cup panko breadcrumbs
½ tsp garlic powder

Salt and black pepper to taste
¼ tsp chipotle seasoning blend
½ cup mayonnaise
1 tsp tabasco chipotle pepper sauce
¼ tsp lemon juice

Directions

In a small bowl, blend well the mayonnaise, tabasco chipotle sauce, lemon juice, and salt. Place in the fridge covered until ready to use. Preheat Cuisinart on Bake function to 390 F.

Slice off the top of the onion, then peel it. Place it cut side down and make 12-16 cuts all around the onion, starting ½ inch from the root. Turn the onion over and gently separate the petals with your fingers so the onion resembles a flower.

Beat the egg lightly with the milk in a bowl. Mix the breadcrumbs, garlic powder, chipotle seasoning, salt, and pepper in a third dish. Dust the onion with the flour, then dip it into the egg wash and coat with the crumbs. Spritz the coated onion with cooking spray.

Place the onion into the greased fryer basket and fit in the baking tray. Cook for 10-12 minutes until crispy and golden brown. Serve with Chipotle mayo on the side.

Parsley Feta Triangles

Prep + Cook Time: 20 minutes | Serves: 4

Ingredients

2 tbsp olive oil
4 oz feta cheese
2 sheets filo pastry
1 egg yolk

2 tbsp parsley, finely chopped
1 scallion, finely chopped
Salt and black pepper to taste

Directions

In a bowl, beat the yolk and mix with feta cheese, parsley, scallion, salt, and black pepper. Cut each filo sheet into three strips. Put a teaspoon of the feta mixture on each strip. Roll the strip in a spinning spiral way until the filling of the inside mixture is wrapped in a triangle.

Preheat Cuisinart on Bake function to 360 F. Brush the surface of filo with olive oil. Arrange the triangles on a greased baking tray and cook for 5 minutes. Lower the temperature to 330 F and cook for 3 more minutes or until golden brown. Serve chilled.

Vegetable Lentil & Bean Loaf

Prep + Cook Time: 65 minutes | Serves: 4

Ingredients

1 (14-ounce) can white beans, drained
1 (14-ounce) can lentils, drained
½ sweet onion, chopped
1 carrot, shredded
1 celery stalk, chopped
1 garlic clove, minced
1 ¼ cups breadcrumbs

2 tbsp flaxseed meal
½ cup vegetable broth
3 tbsp tomato paste
Salt and black pepper to taste
3 tbsp ketchup
2 tbs maple syrup
1 tbsp apple cider vinegar

Directions

Preheat Cuisinart on Bake function to 380 F. Spray a loaf pan with cooking spray. In a blender, place the lentils, white beans, onion, carrot, celery, and garlic and pulse until everything is well incorporated, then pour the mixture into a large bowl. Toss in the breadcrumbs, flaxseed meal, broth, tomato paste, salt, and pepper and stir well. Shape the mixture into the loaf pan.

In a separate bowl, mix the ketchup, maple syrup, and vinegar. Pour the glaze over the lentil loaf. Cook for 50-55 minutes until the top is caramelized and the loaf is solid. Serve sliced.

Vegetable Shepherd's Pie

Prep + Cook Time: 45 minutes | Serves: 6

Ingredients

2 tbsp olive oil
1 ½ pounds mushrooms
1 carrot, diced
1 stalk celery, diced
1 yellow onion, diced
2 garlic cloves, finely chopped
½ tsp dried thyme
1 tbsp flour

1 cup vegetable stock
1 tsp Worcestershire sauce
1 tsp tomato paste
Salt and white pepper to taste
½ cup frozen peas, thawed
1 ½ cups mashed potatoes
2 tbsp parsley, chopped

Directions

Warm the olive oil in a saucepan over medium heat and sauté the mushrooms, carrot, celery, onion, garlic, and thyme for 8-10 minutes until the vegetables are tender.

Stir in the flour for 1-2 minutes. Pour in the stock, Worcestershire sauce, and tomato paste. Reduce the heat to low and simmer for 5-7 minutes, stirring often, until thickened. Adjust the seasoning with salt and white pepper. Stir in the peas and turn the heat off.

Indian-Style Veg Kofta

Prep + Cook Time: 20 minutes | Serves: 4

Ingredients

2 tbsp cornflour
1 cup canned white beans, drained
⅓ cup carrots, grated
2 potatoes, boiled and mashed
¼ cup mint leaves, chopped
½ tsp garam masala powder

½ cup paneer, crumbled
1 Kashmiri chili, minced
1-inch fresh ginger piece, grated
3 garlic cloves, minced
Salt to taste

Directions

Preheat Cuisinart on Air Fry function to 390 F. Place the beans, carrots, garlic, ginger, chili, paneer, and mint in a food processor; process until smooth. Transfer to a bowl. Add in the mashed potatoes, cornflour, salt, and garam masala powder and mix until fully incorporated.

Shape the vegetable mixture into small balls and arrange them on the greased cooking basket. Spritz with cooking oil and cook for 10-12 minutes, turning once, until golden and crispy. Serve.

Mozzarella & Eggplant Sliders

Prep + Cook Time: 15 minutes | Serves: 2

Ingredients

2 hamburger buns
1 eggplant, sliced
½ cup mozzarella cheese, grated
1 red onion, cut into rings

2 lettuce leaves
½ tbsp tomato sauce
1 pickle, sliced

Directions

Preheat Cuisinart on Bake function to 330 F. Place the eggplant slices in a greased baking tray and cook for 6 minutes. Take out the tray and top the eggplants with mozzarella cheese; cook for 1-2 minutes. Spread tomato sauce on the bun bottoms. Place the lettuce on top of the sauce, followed by a cheesy eggplants, onion rings, and pickles. Add the bun tops and serve.

Tomato Cheese Melts

Prep + Cook Time: 20 minutes | Serves: 2

Ingredients

2 tbsp butter, melted
4 white bread slices
2 sharp Cheddar cheese slices

4 tomato slices
2 Gruyère cheese slices
4 fresh basil leaves

Directions

Preheat Cuisinart on Air Fry function to 350 F. Brush all bread slices with butter on both sides. Top two of the slices with cheddar, followed by the tomato, Gruyère cheese, and basil. Cover with the other bread slices. Transfer to the fryer basket and fit in the baking tray.

Cook in the upper position for 10 minutes, flipping once until the tops are golden brown. Remove and let them cool slightly, 1-2 minutes. Slice and serve.

Cheese Spinach Quesadilla

Prep + Cook Time: 20 minutes | Serves: 4

Ingredients

2 tbsp butter
8 corn tortillas, warm
1 cup mozzarella cheese, shredded
1 cup ricotta cheese

1 cup spinach, torn
1 garlic clove, minced
½ cup onions, sliced
½ cup sour cream

Directions

Preheat Cuisinart on Air Fry function to 380 F. Melt the butter in a saucepan over medium heat and sauté garlic and onion for 3 minutes. Stir in spinach and cook for 2-3 more minutes until wilted. Remove from the heat and stir in ricotta cheese, sour cream, and mozzarella cheese.

Divide the spinach mixture between the tortillas. Fold them in half and place them into a baking dish. Cook in your Cuisinart for 8-10 minutes, turning them over halfway through cooking. The quesadillas are done when the tortillas are golden brown and the filling is melted. Serve hot!

Speedy Vegetable Pizza

Prep + Cook Time: 20 minutes | Serves: 1

Ingredients

1 tbsp tomato paste
¼ cup cheddar cheese, grated
¼ cup mozzarella cheese, grated
1 tbsp sweet corn
3 zucchini rounds
3 eggplant rounds

3 red onion rings
½ green bell pepper, chopped
2 cherry tomatoes, quartered
1 pizza crust
¼ tsp basil
¼ tsp oregano

Directions

Preheat Cuisinart on Bake function to 350 F. Spread the tomato paste on the pizza crust. Top with zucchini and eggplant slices, followed by the green peppers and onion rings. Cover with cherry tomatoes and scatter the corn. Sprinkle with oregano and basil and sprinkle with cheddar and mozzarella cheeses. Cook for 10-12 minutes until golden brown on top. Serve and enjoy!

Broccoli & Cheese Egg Ramekins

Prep + Cook Time: 25 minutes | Serves: 4

Ingredients

1 lb broccoli
4 eggs, beaten
½ cup cheddar cheese, shredded
1 cup heavy cream

½ tsp ground nutmeg
1 tsp ginger powder
Salt and black pepper to taste

Directions

In boiling water, steam the broccoli for 5 minutes. Drain and place in a bowl to cool. Mix in the eggs, heavy cream, nutmeg, ginger, salt, and pepper. Divide the mixture between 4 greased ramekins and sprinkle the cheddar cheese on top. Place in a baking tray and cook in your Cuisinart for 10 minutes at 360 F on Bake function. Serve and enjoy!

Parmesan Zucchini Crisps

Prep + Cook Time: 25 minutes | Serves: 4

Ingredients

¼ cup melted butter
4 small zucchini, cut lengthwise
½ cup Parmesan cheese, grated
½ cup breadcrumbs

2 tbsp parsley, chopped
2 garlic cloves, minced
Salt and black pepper to taste

Directions

Preheat Cuisinart on Air Fry function to 350 F. In a bowl, mix breadcrumbs, Parmesan cheese, garlic, parsley, salt, and pepper. Stir in butter. Place the zucchinis cut-side up in a baking tray.

Spread the cheese mixture onto the zucchini evenly. Cook for 13 minutes. Increase the temperature to 370 F and cook for 3 more minutes for extra crunchiness. Serve hot.

Vegetable Spring Rolls

Prep + Cook Time: 15 minutes | Serves: 4

Ingredients

1 tsp olive oil
1 tsp sesame oil
½ head cabbage, grated
2 carrots, grated
1 tsp minced ginger

1 tsp minced garlic
1 tsp soy sauce
1 tsp sesame seeds
½ tsp salt
1 package spring roll wrappers

Directions

Combine all ingredients except for the wrappers in a large bowl. Divide the mixture between the spring roll wrappers and roll them up. Arrange them on a greased baking tray and cook in your Cuisinart for 5 minutes on Bake function at 370 F. Serve and enjoy!

Sweet Potatoes Tater Tots

Prep + Cook Time: 45 minutes | Serves: 4

Ingredients

1 tbsp extra virgin olive oil
1 pound sweet potatoes, peeled and shredded
Salt and black pepper to taste
¼ tsp paprika

½ cup Greek-style yogurt
1 garlic clove, minced
1 tbsp chives, chopped

Directions

In a small bowl, mix the yogurt, olive oil, garlic, chives, and salt and keep in the fridge until ready to serve. Boil the sweet potatoes in salted water over medium heat for 14-16 minutes until almost cooked through. Drain and place in a bowl; let cool for a few minutes.

Preheat Cuisinart on Air Fry function to 400 F. Season the potatoes with salt, pepper, and paprika. Shape the mixture into bite-sized tots. Spritz them with cooking oil and transfer to the greased frying basket. Fit the basket in the baking tray and spray with oil. AirFry in the upper position for 13-15 minutes, turning once until golden and crispy. Serve with yogurt dip.

Vegetable Au Gratin

Prep + Cook Time: 30 minutes | Serves: 3

Ingredients

1 cup eggplants, cubed
¼ cup red peppers, sliced
¼ cup green peppers, sliced
¼ cup onions, chopped
⅓ cup tomatoes, diced
1 clove garlic, minced
1 tbsp pimiento-stuffed olives, sliced

1 tsp capers
¼ tsp dried basil
¼ tsp dried marjoram
Salt and black pepper to taste
¼ cup mozzarella cheese, grated
1 tbsp breadcrumbs

Directions

In a bowl, add eggplants, peppers, onions, tomatoes, olives, garlic, basil, marjoram, capers, salt, and black pepper and mix well. Lightly grease a baking tray with cooking spray. Add in the vegetable mixture and spread it evenly. Sprinkle mozzarella cheese on top and cover with breadcrumbs. Cook in your Cuisinart for 20 minutes on Bake function at 360 F. Serve and enjoy!

Traditional Falafel

Prep + Cook Time: 25 minutes | Serves: 4

Ingredients

1 (15-ounce) can chickpeas, drained
2 spring onions, roughly chopped
3 tbsp chickpea flour
½ tsp baking powder
2 tbsp fresh parsley, chopped
2 tbsp cilantro, chopped
2 garlic cloves, minced
1 tsp ground coriander

1 tsp ground cumin
½ tsp green bell pepper flakes
Salt to taste
⅛ tsp allspice
⅛ tsp cayenne pepper
1 lemon, cut into wedges
½ cup tahini sauce

Directions

Preheat on Air Fry function to 350 F.

Blend all the ingredients, except for the lemon and tahini sauce, until a thick paste is formed in your food processor. Shape into balls and spread out on the frying basket lined with nonstick baking paper. Fit it in the baking tray and spray the falafel with cooking spray on all sides.

Fry until slightly browned, about 15 minutes, shaking the basket once or twice. Serve hot with lemon wedges and tahini sauce on the side.

Korean Tempeh Steak with Broccoli

Prep + Cook Time: 20 minutes + marinating time| Serves: 4

Ingredients

1 tbsp olive oil
2 tbsp sesame oil
16 oz tempeh, cut into 1 cm thick pieces
1 pound broccoli, cut into florets
⅓ cup fermented soy sauce

⅓ cup sherry
1 tsp soy sauce
1 tsp white sugar
1 tsp cornstarch
1 garlic clove, minced

Directions

In a bowl, mix cornstarch, sherry, fermented soy sauce, sesame oil, soy sauce, sugar, and tempeh pieces. Marinate for 45 minutes.

Then, add in garlic, olive oil, and ginger. Place in the basket and fit in the baking tray; cook for 10 minutes at 390 F on Air Fry function, turning once halfway through. Serve.

Preheat Cuisinart on Bake function to 360 F. Transfer the mixture to a baking dish and top with the mashed potatoes. Bake in the lower position 8-12 minutes until the potatoes are golden and crisp and the filling is bubbling. Allow sitting for 5 minutes. Sprinkle with parsley and serve.

Classic Ratatouille

Prep + Cook Time: 80 minutes | Serves: 4

Ingredients

1 tbsp butter, melted
1 zucchini, cut into ½-inch slices
1 eggplant, peeled and cut into ½-inch slices
2 tomatoes, diced
1 red bell peppers, cut into ½-inch chunks
1 green bell peppers, cut into ½-inch chunks
½ yellow onion, chopped

½ cup passata
1 garlic clove, minced
Salt and black pepper to taste
½ tsp Aleppo red pepper flakes
½ tsp green bell pepper flakes
½ cup vegetable broth
½ cup Parmesan cheese, grated

Directions

Preheat Cuisinart on Air Fry function to 360 F. Brush a casserole with melted butter. Add in the zucchini, eggplant, tomatoes, bell peppers, onion, passata, garlic, salt, pepper, red pepper flakes, and green bell pepper flakes and toss to combine. Drizzle the vegetable broth all over.

Cover and seal the casserole with aluminum foil. Bake for 55-60 minutes. Remove the casserole, discard the foil, and sprinkle with Parmesan cheese. Bake for another 5-10 minutes. When the ratatouille is done, the veggies should be soft, and the cheese melted. Serve and enjoy!

Sweetcorn Fritters with Guacamole

Prep + Cook Time: 25 minutes | Serves: 4

Ingredients

1 large avocado, pitted and cored
1 tomato, crushed
½ lime, juiced
½ Jalapeño pepper, seeded and minced
2 cups sweetcorn kernels
2 free-range eggs, lightly beaten
1/3 cup flour

1 tsp baking powder
1 green onion, finely sliced
1 red chili pepper, deseeded and chopped
½ tsp sweet chili sauce
2 tbsp cilantro, chopped
Salt and black pepper to taste

Directions

To make the guacamole: mash the avocado with a fork in a bowl. Add the tomato, lime juice, jalapeño pepper, and mix well. Season with salt and keep in the fridge until ready to serve.

Preheat Cuisinart on Air Fry function to 390 F. In a bowl, combine all the remaining ingredients and mix until a smooth batter forms. Shape the mixture into burger-sized patties and arrange them on the greased fryer basket, spaced apart. Spritz with cooking spray and fit the basket in the baking tray. Bake in the upper position for 14-16 minutes, flipping halfway through until golden and crispy. Serve with prepared guacamole.

Homemade Cheese Ravioli

Prep + Cook Time: 15 minutes | Serves: 4

Ingredients

1 tsp olive oil
1 package cheese ravioli
2 cup Italian breadcrumbs

¼ cup Parmesan cheese, grated
1 cup buttermilk
¼ tsp garlic powder

Directions

Preheat Cuisinart on Air Fry function to 390 F. In a small bowl, combine breadcrumbs, Parmesan cheese, garlic powder, and olive oil. Dip the ravioli in the buttermilk and then coat them with the breadcrumb mixture.

Line the Air Fryer pan with parchment paper and arrange the ravioli on it. Cook for 5 minutes. Serve the ravioli with marinara sauce.

Coconut Vegan Fries

Prep + Cook Time: 20 minutes | Serves: 2

Ingredients

2 tbsp olive oil
2 tbsp coconut oil
2 potatoes, spiralized

1 tbsp tomato ketchup
Salt and black pepper to taste

Directions

In a bowl, mix olive oil, coconut oil, salt, and pepper. Add in the potatoes and toss to coat. Place them in the basket and fit in the baking tray; cook for 15 minutes on Air Fry function at 360 F. Serve with ketchup and enjoy!

Garlicky Vermouth Mushrooms

Prep + Cook Time: 20 minutes | Serves: 4

Ingredients

1 tbsp olive oil
1 tbsp duck fat, softened
2 lb portobello mushrooms, sliced

2 tbsp vermouth
½ tsp garlic powder
2 tsp herbs

Directions

In a bowl, mix the duck fat, garlic powder, and herbs. Rub the mushrooms with the mixture and place them in a baking tray. Drizzle with vermouth and olive oil and cook in your Cuisinart for 15 minutes on Bake function at 350 F. Serve and enjoy!

DESSERTS

Summer Citrus Sponge Cake

Prep + Cook Time: 40 minutes | Serves: 4

Ingredients

1 cup butter
1 cup sugar
1 cup self-rising flour
3 eggs

1 tsp baking powder
1 tsp vanilla extract
Zest of 1 orange

Frosting:
4 egg whites
1 orange, zested and juiced

1 tsp orange food coloring
1 cup superfine sugar

Directions

Preheat Cuisinart on Bake function to 350 F. Place all cake ingredients in a bowl and whisk with an electric mixer. Transfer the batter into a greased cake pan and bake for 25-30 minutes until golden brown and a toothpick inserted comes out dry and clean.

Meanwhile, prepare the frosting by beating all frosting ingredients together. Spread the frosting mixture on top of the cake. Serve sliced.

Dark Chocolate Lava Cakes

Prep + Cook Time: 30 minutes | Serves: 4

Ingredients

8 tbsp butter
6 oz dark chocolate
2 egg yolks
2 eggs
4 tbsp sugar

1 ½ tbsp flour
¼ tsp salt
1 tbsp orange zest
2 tbsp chocolate powder

Directions

Preheat Cuisinart on Bake function to 350 F. Microwave the chocolate and butter for 60-90 seconds, stir to combine; let cool slightly. In a bowl, whisk the egg yolks, eggs, and sugar until frothy. Add the chocolate mixture, flour, salt, and orange zest and blend until smooth.

Grease 4 ramekins with cooking spray and dust with some cocoa powder. Spoon the batter into the ramekins. Tap the ramekins on the counter a few times to prevent air bubbles. Place into the baking tray cook in the lower position for 15 minutes. Let cool for 2 minutes before turning the cakes upside down onto serving plates.

Mini Apple Pies

Prep + Cook Time: 30 minutes | Serves: 4

Ingredients

2 oz butter, melted
4 apples, diced
2 oz sugar
1 oz brown sugar

2 tsp cinnamon
1 egg, beaten
3 large puff pastry sheets
¼ tsp salt

Directions

Whisk white sugar, brown sugar, cinnamon, salt, and butter together in a bowl. Place the apples in a greased baking pan and coat them with the sugar mixture. Place the baking dish in your Cuisinart and cook for 10 minutes at 350 F on Bake function.

Meanwhile, roll out the pastry on a floured flat surface and cut each sheet into 6 equal pieces. Divide the apple filling between the pieces. Brush the edges of the pastry squares with the egg.

Fold them and seal the edges with a fork. Place on a lined baking sheet and cook in the fryer at 350 F for 8 minutes. Flip over, increase the temperature to 390 F, and cook for 2 more minutes.

Perfect Chocolate Soufflé

Prep + Cook Time: 30 minutes | Serves: 2

Ingredients

¼ cup butter, melted
2 eggs, whites and yolks separated
2 tbsp flour

3 tbsp sugar
3 oz chocolate, melted
½ tsp vanilla extract

Directions

Beat the yolks along with the sugar and vanilla extract; stir in butter, chocolate, and flour. Preheat Cuisinart on Bake function to 330 F. Whisk the whites until a stiff peak forms. Working in batches, gently combine the egg whites with the chocolate mixture. Divide the batter between two greased ramekins. Cook for 14-18 minutes. Serve.

Homemade Doughnuts

Prep + Cook Time: 25 minutes | Serves: 4

Ingredients

2 ½ tbsp butter
8 oz self-rising flour
1 tsp baking powder

½ cup milk
1 egg
2 oz brown sugar

Directions

Preheat Cuisinart on Bake function to 350 F. Beat the butter with the sugar until smooth. Whisk in the egg and milk. In a bowl, combine flour with baking powder. Fold in the butter mixture. Form donut shapes and cut off the center with cookie cutters. Arrange on a lined baking sheet and cook in for 15 minutes. Serve with whipped cream or icing.

Glazed Lemon Cupcakes

Prep + Cook Time: 30 minutes | Serves: 6

Ingredients

2 tbsp vegetable oil	¾ tsp baking powder
1 cup flour	¼ tsp baking soda
½ cup sugar	½ tsp salt
1 small egg	½ cup milk
1 tsp lemon zest	½ tsp vanilla extract

Glaze:

½ cup powdered sugar	2 tsp lemon juice

Directions

Preheat Cuisinart on Bake function to 350 F. In a bowl, combine dry ingredients. In another bowl, whisk together the wet ingredients. Gently combine the two mixtures. Divide the batter between 6 greased muffin tins. Place them in the baking tray and cook for 13-16 minutes.

Meanwhile, whisk the powdered sugar with lemon juice. Spread the glaze over the muffins.

Vanilla Almond Meringue

Prep + Cook Time: 100 minutes + cooling time| Serves: 4

Ingredients

8 egg whites	2 tsp lemon juice
½ tsp almond extract	1 ½ tsp vanilla extract
1 ⅓ cups sugar	Melted dark chocolate for garnish

Directions

In a bowl, add egg whites and lemon juice. Beat using an electric mixer until foamy. Slowly add the sugar and continue beating until completely combined; stir in almond and vanilla extracts.

Line the Air Fryer pan with parchment paper. Fill a piping bag with the meringue mixture and pipe as many mounds on the baking pan as you can, leaving 2-inch spaces between each mound. Cook at 240 F for 80-90 minutes on Bake function until set and a little golden. Let cool for 2 hours. Drizzle with dark chocolate and serve.

Classic Pecan Pie

Prep + Cook Time: 45 minutes | Serves: 4

Ingredients

1 tbsp butter, melted
¾ cup maple syrup
2 eggs
½ tsp salt
¼ tsp nutmeg
½ tsp cinnamon

2 tbsp almond butter
2 tbsp brown sugar
½ cup chopped pecans
1 8-inch pie dough
¾ tsp vanilla extract

Directions

Preheat Cuisinart on Toast function to 350 F. Coat the pecans with the melted butter. Place the pecans in a baking tray and toast them for 5 minutes. Press the pie crust into a baking pan, crimping the top edges if desired and scatter the pecans over.

Whisk together all remaining ingredients in a bowl. Pour the mixture over the pecans. Set Cuisinart to 320 F and cook the pie for 25-30 minutes on Bake function.

Sesame Banana Dessert

Prep + Cook Time: 15 minutes | Serves: 5

Ingredients

1 ½ cups flour
5 bananas, sliced
1 tsp salt
3 tbsp sesame seeds

1 cup water
2 eggs, beaten
1 tsp baking powder
½ tbsp sugar

Directions

Preheat Cuisinart on Bake function to 340 F. In a bowl, mix salt, sesame seeds, flour, baking powder, eggs, sugar, and water. Coat sliced bananas with the flour mixture. Place the prepared slices in the fryer basket and fit in the baking tray; cook for 8-10 minutes. Serve chilled.

Honey Hazelnut Apples

Prep + Cook Time: 40 minutes | Serves: 4

Ingredients

1 oz butter
4 apples
2 oz breadcrumbs
Zest of 1 orange

2 tbsp chopped hazelnuts
2 oz mixed seeds
1 tsp cinnamon
2 tbsp honey

Directions

Preheat Cuisinart on Bake function to 350 F. Core the apples. Combine the remaining ingredients in a bowl; stuff the apples with the mixture and cook for 25-30 minutes. Serve and enjoy!

Chocolate Banana Bread

Prep + Cook Time: 80 minutes | Serves: 6

Ingredients

½ cup butter, melted
1 tbsp raisins, soaked
1 cup flour + for dusting the pan
½ cup dark brown sugar
¼ cup cocoa powder
2 tsp baking powder

¼ tsp salt
2 bananas, mashed
1 fresh egg
1 tsp vanilla extract
½ cup dark chocolate chips
2 tbsp powdered sugar

Directions

Preheat Cuisinart on Bake function to 330 F. Beat the egg with the butter and vanilla in a bowl. Add in the mashed bananas and stir to combine. In another bowl, sift the flour, baking powder, cocoa powder, and salt. Stir and mix in the brown sugar. Combine the wet and dry ingredients and stir well, then pour in the dark chocolate chips and raisins and stir again.

Pour the batter into a greased loaf pan and cook for 60 minutes or until a toothpick inserted comes out dry and clean. Allow the bread to sit for 10 minutes. Use a knife to loosen the bread from the pan, then set the bread on a rack. Serve topped with powdered sugar after it cools a bit.

Quick Coffee Cake

Prep + Cook Time: 40 minutes | Serves: 4

Ingredients

½ cup butter, melted
1 tsp instant coffee
2 tbsp black coffee, brewed
2 eggs

½ cup sugar
1 cup flour
1 tsp cocoa powder
Powdered sugar for icing

Directions

Preheat Cuisinart on Bake function to 360 F. Beat the sugar, butter, and eggs together in a bowl. Add the cocoa, instant and black coffees, and flour to a separate bowl and stir to combine. Add in the wet mixture and whisk until well combined. Spoon the batter into a greased cake pan. Cook for 25-30 minutes. Dust with powdered sugar and serve chilled.

Easy Berry Crumble

Prep + Cook Time: 30 minutes | Serves: 6

Ingredients

6 tbsp cold butter, cubed
2 cups fresh strawberries
1 cup fresh raspberries

1 cup fresh blueberries
1 tsp lemon zest
½ tsp vanilla extract

1 cup flour
1 tbsp cornstarch
½ cup sugar

Directions

Preheat Cuisinart on Bake function to 350 F. In a bowl, place half of the sugar, cornstarch, and lemon zest and stir to combine. Add the vanilla and berries; toss to coat. Gently mash the berries, but make sure there are chunks left. Place the berry mixture in a greased cake pan.

Combine the flour and remaining sugar in a bowl. Add the cold butter. Rub the butter with your fingers until the mixture becomes crumbled. Spread the mixture over the berries. Bake for 15 minutes until the filling is bubbling and the top is browned. Serve chilled.

Gluten-Free Fried Bananas

Prep + Cook Time: 20 minutes | Serves: 6

Ingredients

3 tbsp vegetable oil
8 bananas
3 tbsp cornflour

1 egg white
¾ cup breadcrumbs

Directions

Preheat Cuisinart on Toast function to 350 F. Combine the oil and breadcrumbs in a small bowl. Coat the bananas with the cornflour first, brush them with egg white, and dip them in the breadcrumb mixture. Arrange on a lined baking sheet and cook for 8-12 minutes. Serve.

Authentic Raisin Apple Treat

Prep + Cook Time: 45 minutes | Serves: 4

Ingredients

4 apples, cored
1 ½ oz almonds

¾ oz raisins
2 tbsp sugar

Directions

Preheat Cuisinart on Bake function to 360 F. In a bowl, mix the sugar, almonds, and raisins. Fill cored apples with the mixture. Place the apples into a greased baking tray and cook for 30-35 minutes. Serve with a sprinkle of powdered sugar if desired.

Made in the USA
Columbia, SC
19 June 2021

40465218R00061